PARTNERS IN CHRIST

A Conservative Case for Egalitarianism

JOHN G. STACKHOUSE, JR.

IVP Academic

An imprint of InterVarsity Press
Downers Grove, Illinois

InterVarsity Press
P.O. Box 1400, Downers Grove, IL 60515-1426
ivpress.com
email@ivpress.com

InterVarsity Press® is the book-publishing division of InterVarsity Christian Fellowship/USA®, a movement of students and faculty active on campus at hundreds of universities, colleges and schools of nursing in the United States of America, and a member movement of the International Fellowship of Evangelical Students. For information about local and regional activities, visit intervarsity.org.

Scripture quotations, unless otherwise noted, are from the New Revised Standard Version of the Bible, copyright 1989 by the Division of Christian Education of the National Council of the Churches of Christ in the USA. Used by permission. All rights reserved.

While any stories in this book are true, some names and identifying information may have been changed to protect the privacy of individuals.

Substantial material in this book is taken from John G. Stackhouse, Jr., Finally Feminist: A Pragmatic Christian Understanding of Gender (Grand Rapids: Baker Academic, a division of Baker Publishing Group, 2005). Used by permission.

Cover design: David Fassett
Interior design: Beth McGill
Images: © dicus63/iStockphoto

ISBN 978-0-8308-4081-6 (print)
ISBN 978-0-8308-9894-7 (digital)

Printed in the United States of America ∞

Library of Congress Cataloging-in-Publication Data

Stackhouse, John G. (John Gordon), 1960-
  Partners in Christ : a conservative case for egalitarianism / John G. Stackhouse, Jr.
     pages cm
  Includes bibliographical references and index.
  ISBN 978-0-8308-4081-6 (pbk. : alk. paper)
  1. Sex role--Religious aspects--Christianity. I. Title.
  BT708.S674 2015
  270.082--dc23

                                                                              2015027320

P	24	23	22	21	20	19	18	17	16	15	14	13	12	11	10	9	8	7	6	5	4	3	2	1
Y	35	34	33	32	31	30	29	28	27	26	25	24	23	22	21	20	19	18	17	16	15

For my sister Cindra,

and her husband, Daniel,

who have shown over the years

what I in this book

try to tell

Contents

Whose Side Are You On?

LET'S BEGIN OUR DISCUSSION OF GENDER the way any Christian discussion ought to begin: with Jesus. I love Jesus, and I expect you do too. If you don't (yet), you're certainly welcome to keep reading. But in this book I am primarily addressing a reader who already is committed to the Christian faith, and thus is personally committed to Jesus.

To begin this way is neither truistic nor trivial. Far too many discussions of gender have disappeared almost instantly down one or both of the following slippery slopes into hellish excommunication. Here's the first one:

"You say you believe that women should preach?"

"Yes, I do."

"Well, the Bible clearly says that they shouldn't. You therefore don't believe the Bible . . . which is the Word of God . . . and therefore you don't believe God . . . and so you aren't a Christian, but instead are a wolf in sheep's clothing that must be unmasked and denounced as such."

Whew.

Here's the second slippery slope:

"You say you believe that women should *not* preach?"

"Yes, I do."

"Well, the Bible clearly says that they should. You therefore don't believe the Bible . . . which is the Word of God . . . and therefore you don't believe God . . . and so you aren't a Christian, but instead are a wolf in sheep's clothing that must be unmasked and denounced as such."

Instead, then, of immediately consigning our opponents to the lake of fire, let's remember Jesus. Let's remember that we love Jesus. Let's remember that we're trying to understand Jesus, and worship Jesus, and obey Jesus, and become like Jesus, and share Jesus the very best that we can. If we're in a debate over a Christian view of gender with someone who is not serious about Jesus, of course, then we have to have a different kind of debate. And we are all sinners, so we have to allow for the fact that each of us Christians will inevitably bring to this discussion our various memories and worries and agendas—not all of which, to put it extremely kindly, conform precisely to the will of God. We can and we must, however, presume goodwill, and goodwill of the most basic Christian sort: we're trying to follow Jesus. You are. I am.

So let's grant each other that identity and proceed as if we really meant it—as brothers and sisters, fellow disciples, and coworkers in the global enterprise of God's redemption of the world. I hope I will sound, throughout this book, like I'm a Christian and like I believe you are too. And I hope you will respond to what I say in like spirit. We're agreed on the Main Things: the fundamental doctrines of the faith (as particularly listed in the great creeds); the supreme authority of the Bible as God's Word written; the necessity of conversion; the teaching and sanctifying ministry of the Holy Spirit; and the other basics of orthodox, traditional, mainstream Christianity. I happen to identify myself—albeit gingerly, depending on my audience—with evangelical Protestantism. But there is nothing in what follows that depends on any evangelical peculiarities (of which, alas, there are far too many). So if you're a faithful Christian of whatever stripe, you ought to feel at home in this conversation.[1]

I presume also that you are an intelligent person, just as I assume that my theological counterparts generally are intelligent people. Another one of the chief ways in which Christian discussion of gender goes sideways is for one side or the other (and often both) to start condescending to the other as stupid children who do not understand how to do theology properly: they lack the requisite scholarly knowledge to interpret the Bible aright, or they fail to appreciate the theological implications of their exegesis, or they do not see the social implications of their views, or they simply cannot reason validly.

I have not found it useful to presume that my counterparts in any conversation were either wicked or witless. Alas, of course, some have proved to be one or the other, or both. But in this particular discussion, I have found things to be quite the other way: vast amounts of time have been spent in careful analysis of a wide range of texts; impressive arguments have been mounted that range across the whole Bible; two thousand years of church history and theological tradition have been surveyed; and social, political, psychological, and sexual implications have been considered—and on *both* sides of the issue. It seems evident to me that the way to best find our way through the gender debate is not to presume that we will eventually discover that one set of discussants or the other are immoral morons. Instead, I much prefer to think that we can find a way to do honor to both groups of our fellow Christians. Shall we try?

LABELS: WHO'S WHO

Let's start with some basic identifications. Usually this discussion is conducted in terms of two polar opposites: patriarchy ("rule by the father") on one side and feminism ("advocacy for women") on the other. Let's pause for just a moment to acknowledge that there have been, in fact, a number of intermediate positions in Christian history: female missionaries, church planters, campus staff workers, and the like who were not allowed to exercise pastoral functions at home but were welcome to engage in them on this or that "mission field"; female preachers during boundary-blurring revivals who, once the excitement had cooled down, were then shepherded out of the pulpit and back into the pew; and female Bible teachers, preachers, and authors who conducted extensive ministry officially "under" the authority of a husband, or pastor, or church.[2]

Coherent theologies have not generally been elaborated to defend

such practices, however. Instead, the main attention has been given
to the two typical alternatives: patriarchalism, which has been renamed in America and elsewhere "complementarianism," and feminism, which has been similarly renamed "egalitarianism." Let's take
a few moments to be clear about what we mean by these terms, as we
shall use them in the rest of this discussion.

First, consider the "f-word" that has become odious not only
among many Christians but also among many people in society at
large—even, and sometimes especially, among young women who
might be presumed to be feminists. Indeed, substantively most of
them are in fact feminists, as we shall see. But the word evokes now
an ugly stereotype of lesbian misanthropes or perhaps wickedly al-
luring sexual predators who threaten the integrity of the family, sexual
purity, masculinity, and yes, civilization itself, in the eyes of the most
frightened. Many of my own university students could easily agree
with almost any standard set of feminist tenets but would horrifiedly
eschew the label. "I don't hate men!" a few have confided in me. "I'm
no feminist!"[3]

How can one possibly, therefore, be a Christian feminist? For many
people, obviously, "Christian feminist" is a contradiction in terms.
And it isn't just the exaggerated specter of feminism that Christians
fear. For many Christians today, it is just axiomatic that true believers
believe in patriarchy—in "male leadership" in church and home, if
not also in society at large. And most Christians have, in fact, so believed—regardless of age, race, class, or gender, across hundreds of
cultures and two thousand years. It is a matter of simple fact that most
Christians still do believe in patriarchy, as one recalls that the majority of Christians live outside the so-called developed countries in
which feminism has made its inroads. And it is obvious, furthermore,
that within those developed countries—and perhaps conspicuously
in the largest and most influential of these, the United States of
America—many Christians of almost every denominational stripe
continue to believe that the Bible and Christian tradition just obviously command the submission of women to the authority of men in

marriage and in the church, if not, again, also in society.

Feminism is thus a plague on the land, related as it has been to a wide range of social pathologies. Feminism obviously has been implicated in the so-called sexual liberation of women—both in terms of liberal mores (women are free to be as promiscuous as men have been) and of controversial reproductive technologies (the Pill and the ready and legal availability of abortion). Feminism has been coupled with radical changes in the public workplace that have brought many women into jobs outside the home, including jobs previously dominated by men. This availability of female labor has been blamed for the depression of wages and loss of benefits in many occupations that previously paid a "living wage" for a man and his family. Feminism has been held responsible for children having to go to daycare or let themselves in to their homes in the afternoon with their "latchkeys" because both parents are working outside the home—or, worse, because the parents are divorced and the single parent is still at work. Feminism has been linked with lesbianism and the rise of homosexual activism—and the very arguments used to support female clergy are now used to support homosexuals in the pulpit as well. Finally, feminism has given voice to hatred for the Christian church and its Scriptures, as feminists have traced the oppression of women in our culture particularly to the patriarchy endorsed by Christian teaching through the ages.

So to suggest combining "Christian" with "feminist" strikes many of our contemporaries as both intellectually preposterous and morally outrageous—from both the traditional Christian and, ironically enough, the radical feminist points of view.

I have responded to this situation from two, apparently opposed, directions. On the one hand, I am a white, middle-class, heterosexual, evangelical Christian man—and thus departing rather markedly from the feminist stereotype. Indeed, one might think that I would have a lot to lose in supporting the equal treatment of women in every sphere of life—whether one sees that loss as my "legitimate authority" or my "scandalous privilege." On the other hand, I am also a career academician: someone who has earned degrees from two secular universities, has held appointments at three more and has had books published by the presses of yet two others. Someone with that sort of mainstream scholarly background can be expected to be a feminist, of course. But one might not expect such a person to be an orthodox Bible-believer.

In this book, then, I will try to show how one can be both authentically feminist and authentically Christian. In particular, I will try to show how the Bible, which has often been understood by *both* feminists and patriarchalists to be inimical to feminism, properly can be seen instead to support feminism in our time.[4]

I recognize that the noun *feminist* can mean several things, but this is what I mean by it: someone who champions the dignity, rights, responsibilities, and glories of women as equal in importance to those of men, and who therefore refuses discrimination against women. Thus, in this book *feminist* and *egalitarian* are synonyms. Yes, women and men are biologically different, and so some sex-specific zones are obviously real and therefore not arbitrary.[5] And I also believe that the universal folk wisdom is true: men and women differ also in other essential ways, although there is currently nothing approaching a modern consensus as to what those ways are. (We will return to the question of "gender essentialism" in due course.) Feminists, then, are not blind to real differences and their implications. Quite the contrary: many feminists emphasize that women and men are indeed different, and a large part of the feminist concern is that those differences ought to be recognized and incorporated creatively and respectfully into our life together.[6] Feminists of the sort I represent are those who resist what they judge to be *arbitrary, ungrounded* distinctions between men and women and the discrimination that attends such distinctions.[7]

Those on the other side of this Christian debate are called "traditionalists," "patriarchalists," and other, sometimes less flattering, names. The term many of them now prefer is *complementarians*, reflecting their contention that both women and men are fully human and reflect the image of God, but are sometimes called by God to different, and "complementary," roles on the basis of their sex. Furthermore, when social power is in view (as opposed to, say, the power to bear children), then men and women complement each other in that men normally are to wield power—beneficently, to be sure—and women normally are to subordinate themselves to it as, indeed, an ordinance of God.

Many have observed that the terms *complementarian* and *egalitarian* in fact can be applied to aspects of each side's viewpoint. Egalitarians do not deny gender differences that complement each other, complementarians affirm the essential equality of women and men, and so on. Acknowledging that ambiguity, we nonetheless still need labels, and none better have yet emerged. So we will use them in what is still the common sense of each.[8]

2

How *Not* to Decide About Gender

MANY AUTHORS ON THE QUESTION of Christianity and gender begin with the broader context of hermeneutics—the discipline of interpreting the Bible and applying it to contemporary issues.[1] It's actually quite remarkable, however, that many do not, but instead immediately plunge into exegetical and historical issues as if we all engage in theological reasoning the same way and there are no important methodological questions to sort out first. But as Pamela Dickey Young reminds us, "One's theological method in large part determines one's theological outcome."[2] If one generally assumes, for example, that Old Testament law is to apply to Christians today directly and without adaptation, then one will be led to certain conclusions about gender. If one assumes that the portraits of Jesus in the Gospels are the final interpretative norm in Scripture, then one will necessarily entertain only a certain range of interpretative options. And if one assumes that contemporary natural and social science do, or do not, shed important light on the matters they discuss, then one will see questions of gender differently.

Before I offer what hermeneutical wisdom I possess pertinent to our subject, let me begin by discussing common ways people deal *badly* with the question of gender.[3]

Many people, it seems, are impatient with discussion of methodology when the issue of gender arises. Maybe you're feeling that way now! Indeed, lots of sensible Christians don't understand why it has to arise at all. They believe that the question of whether Christianity is compatible with gender egalitarianism has already been resolved—and resolved easily. Some, of course, believe it has been resolved in favor of compatibility, as in "Of course Christians can be feminists!" Others believe it has been resolved in favor of mutual exclusivity: "You're either a genuine Christian or a feminist—you can't be both."

The controversy, however, continues. And my point here is that it cannot be settled, as some content themselves that it can, merely by recourse to one of three favorite interpretative shortcuts: Biblicism, reference to the common wisdom of contemporary society, and personal intuition.

BIBLICISM: "THE BIBLE SAYS SO"

There is a longstanding form of Christian piety, commonly found especially among Protestants, that congratulates itself for its fidelity to the Bible against all other voices. "No creed but the Bible," they will proclaim, or perhaps "*Sola Scriptura*," if they like to add the gloss of tradition and the aura of Latin. Other plainspoken people merely declare, "The Bible says it; I believe it; that settles it." Yet such Bible-believing Christians are fooling themselves when they claim to interpret and practice simply "what the Bible says."

For one thing, they are failing to realize that it is their own interpretations that they are defending, not the Bible itself. Indeed, so great is their confidence that they can simply read the Bible—a compilation of dozens of ancient books, composed originally in now-dead languages that no one can even confidently pronounce, from a variety of countries, authors, and contexts—that such people are surprised and even offended when one indicates that they merely possess their own *interpretation* of this complicated literature, not its full and final meaning.

Folk piety among such Christians often affirms that the Bible is so clear that a little child can read it. (Occasionally one finds this idea dressed up as affirmation of "the perspicuity of Scripture.") Like much of folklore generally, this assertion is partly true and also importantly false. Yes, someone of very limited intellectual ability can hear or read the Bible and be blessed by its profound simplicities: "God is love," "You shall have no other gods before me," "Jesus is Lord," and so on. But God gave his people teachers, as the Bible itself affirms, precisely because much of the Bible is *not* easily understood. How is it that God is love . . . and yet my life is plagued by suffering? There aren't any other gods, so why is this commandment still relevant, if it is? And what does it mean—in politics, yes, but also in economics, business, family life, and so on—that "Jesus is Lord"? Ah, now we need something more than childlike faith: we need adult reflection.

Some people of this outlook occasionally claim sophisticated company with champions such as Tertullian ("I believe because it is absurd") and Søren "Leap of Faith" Kierkegaard. But these notables are among the few eminent Christians who can be invoked in such a cause. And even then they are misunderstood. For these were Christian thinkers who valued reason so much that they employed quite a lot of it in their several theological writings. Like the apostle Paul himself, who is occasionally invoked in this regard (so 1 Cor 1:18-31), these great Christian thinkers opposed intellectual *vanity* and dependence on wisdom other than God's. They had no quarrel with reason, philosophy, and other intellectual disciplines when *rightly* deployed in God's service.

Instead, we should value all of God's intellectual gifts to us. God has given us experience—spiritual experience, yes, but also all of the wide experiences of the wide world. God has given us tradition—Christian tradition, yes, but also all of the traditions of the various groups and communities and institutions that have shaped us. God has given us scholarship—Christian scholarship, yes, but also the "wealth of the Egyptians" (Augustine) and "the best that has been thought and said" (Matthew Arnold). God has given us art—Christian art, yes, but also the insight and imagination of artists great and small. None of these resources, of course, are infallible—as Scripture is. But all of them help us understand our world and perform our God-given tasks in it, so we rightly consult them as we decide about any matter of importance.

To be sure, Scripture is the privileged member of this set: No Christian can safely decide against what he or she understands Scripture to say, since God has specially blessed Scripture as his written revelation. Still, because we are human beings with limited intellectual capacities and, worse, we are still subject to the influence of sin, we must beware of our interpretations of *anything*, including Scripture, as at least *possibly* mistaken and maybe even self-serving. God thus gives us a variety of "checks and balances" in these various resources. It is not, then, especially pious to refuse to use what God has given us in experience, tradition, scholarship, and art in favor of an exclusive use of Scripture. To do so is, instead, both foolish and ungrateful.

There are sophisticated forms of this ungrateful foolishness apparent in the Christian gender debate. Time and again, defenders of patriarchy will campaign on the grounds that "the Bible says so," as if that should suffice. But if what *we think* the Bible says (that is, our interpretation) seems contrary to one or more of the other intellectual resources God has given us, should we not pause to consider whether we have made a mistake somewhere—perhaps in our interpretation of secular reason or spiritual experience, yes, but also perhaps in our interpretation of the Bible? The Bible might well contradict secular reason or one's spiritual experience. Indeed, it often has done so. But it often also has not, and the God of all truth expects us to weigh interpretation against interpretation in the light of all we think we know, as adults do—with humble recognition especially of the human penchant for glorifying a preferred way of seeing things by dressing it up in religious legitimations.

Particularly as we are deciding about the emotionally and politically charged issue of gender distinctions, we should pause to consider a general characteristic of God's Word. God speaks not only what is "right," but also what is "good." Let's hear again the familiar words of Psalm 19:7-9:

> The law of the LORD is perfect,
>   reviving the soul;
> the decrees of the LORD are sure,
>   making wise the simple;

the precepts of the LORD are right,
　　rejoicing the heart;
the commandment of the LORD is clear,
　　enlightening the eyes;
the fear of the LORD is pure,
　　enduring forever;
the ordinances of the LORD are true
　　and righteous altogether.

The Psalmist commends God's Word not as merely "divine command"—to be obeyed whether or not it appears to be good—but as transparently commendable wisdom on grounds appreciable by all. God's law appeals to us as healthy, strong, informative, joyful, corrective, holy, and so on. Normally, then, when God commands something, we can see why it makes sense for him to do so. His written Word normally does not contradict, but rather illuminates and harmonizes with, his self-expression in other media, whether our experience, our tradition, and so on. To be sure, sometimes God's Word comes to us as a rebuke to sinful errors, or as a corrective to our hapless mistakes. But even then we are equipped by the Spirit to recognize it as God's Word and as true and good.

So when it comes to the question of gender, we can properly ask ourselves, Why is this commandment of the Lord *good*, as well as right? For if our interpretation of God's Word seems to result in something *bad*, it may be that it is our own badness that is being confronted and needs reorientation, but it may also be that we have interpreted God's good Word literally *badly*.

As a sort of "diagnostic test," then, perhaps we can consider these "sentence stems" to see whether they illuminate one or another interpretation of gender as good or bad:

"It is better for church government to have only men and no women because . . ."

"It is better to listen only to male preachers and never to female preachers because . . ."

"It is better for all church meetings for men always to lead in prayer, the liturgy, music, and so on, and no women ever to lead in any of those zones, because . . ."

"It is important always to make sure a woman who does participate in public worship to have a man 'over her' in some authoritative role because . . ."

Can these stems be completed patriarchally in any way that makes sense besides "because the Bible [as we interpret it] says so"?

Again, I want to affirm that in any given case God's Word may be calling us to change our minds, to revise our expectations, to reframe issues that we have sinfully or at least confusedly misunderstood. But it also may be that as we use our God-given reason, drawing on the experiences God has given us, we will not defy God's Word, but instead come to understand it better and thus purge ourselves of erroneous interpretations.

In this regard, then, it seems to me that the burden of proof falls on the complementarians. They are obliged to show how it is really better for subordination to continue to characterize the relationship of Christian men and women, rather than just banging on about "the Bible says . . ."—again, *not* to subordinate the Bible to human reason (let alone human preference!), but as a *check* on their *interpretation* of God's authoritative Word.

CULTURAL CONFORMITY—OR NONCONFORMITY: "SOCIETY SAYS SO, AND THEREFORE WE SHOULD—"

Our society's values cannot be assumed to be fully right. Does anyone doubt that? Our society has previously taught us lots of things that we now think are wrong: that women are not entitled to legal or political recognition; that people of other ethnic groups are eligible for exploitation; that the poor are not entitled to assistance; and so on. Our society has said that governmental sponsorship of religion is good, then sometimes good, then bad. And so on.

Nor, however, can our society's values be assumed to be wrong, as many alienated conservative Christians seem to feel, since many of our society's values have in fact emerged from a Christian cultural matrix. Furthermore, many other religions and philosophies share at least some values with the Bible, so there is often common ground upon which to make common cause.

We therefore cannot simply use ethical reasoning in the form of "Society currently says *x*, and therefore *x* is right." Nor can we say the opposite: ". . . and therefore *x* is wrong." The world is a place of ideological contest, in which forces of good and evil contend and in which, as Aleksandr Solzhenitsyn said, the dividing line of good and evil is drawn right through our own hearts—both individually and corporately. There is no entirely bad society on record and there is no entirely good one, either. We must exercise discernment ad hoc, taking each case on its own terms and seeking God's enlightenment as to what is his will in this instance.[4]

Thus when it comes to the matter of gender, we must not unreflectively assume that what society says about women and men is right. Society might be wrong. And, for another thing, let's recognize that "society" is not speaking with a single voice about gender nowadays. Women are executives, yes, but also regularly portrayed as bimbos (and worse) in popular culture. Women are leaders, yes, but when they want to be mothers also, North American society has yet to accommodate them well. Women and men are "just the same" and also profoundly and universally different. It's not actually clear just what contemporary society is, in fact, saying about gender.

Furthermore, society says a number of other things in this sphere and related ones that most Christians believe are highly questionable, if not downright false: that homosexuality is natural and normal; that sexual intercourse can be merely recreational; that cohabiting is a good preparation for marriage; that amicable divorces are better for children than unhappy marriages; and so on.

Yet it is good for us to recognize also that modern society has in many respects come to speak more "Christianly"—or, more accurately, more in line with the Bible as a whole—than it did in ostensibly more Christian days. Compare today with a hundred years ago, and ask yourself whether we have improved how we treat handicapped people, people of other ethnicities and religions, and the unemployed. Godly values are, indeed, still evident and even growing in some sectors of contemporary life—the worldwide spread of the language of "universal human rights" is a great trend forward—at the same time as other biblical values seem to be eroding.

When it comes, then, to reflecting on any issue, we cannot take our cues automatically—whether positively or negatively—from what our society happens to be doing or saying today. We have to do our own homework, and see what Christ is saying to the church in our place and time.

INTUITION: "THE SPIRIT SAYS SO"

Because church tradition, societal practice, and the heritage of biblical interpretation all seemed against them, many women seeking greater freedom in Christian service have relied on their inner sense of God's leading. These women were not always radicals in the heat of evangelical revivals, or in the institutions of medieval monasticism, or in the netherworld of the cults (what we more politely refer to nowadays as "new religious movements"). These women show up as respectable nuns, missionaries, Bible teachers, evangelists, and authors throughout church history. And when they have been called on to account for their ministry, as they rarely have been, many of them have responded, "The Lord led me to it."[5]

This reliance on spiritual discernment, whatever its good fruit, is dangerous, as many of these women recognized. One's personal intuitions—even, or perhaps especially, those that we think are from God—must be tested against the alternative possibilities of self-deception, demonic deception, and just plain misunderstanding (e.g., excessive or misguided application of a genuinely true Word of God). The history of mysticism is replete with cautions and safeguards offered by spiritual masters who are well aware of the perils of misinterpreted experience. And mainstream Christian teaching affirms that one's intuitive sense of God's voice should be matched up with Scripture, tradition, and reason—and in the company of other Christians—so as to minimize the danger of misunderstanding or misdirection and to maximize the blessing of a genuine divine communication.

In an extreme situation, to be sure, the Christian can be grateful for a compelling intuition: there is no Scripture or church tradition that immediately pertains to the question at hand, the believer has no access to scholarship or to other Christians with relevant competence to share, and so on. But in the current debate, there is little excuse for relying on sheer intuition when the theological resources are so extensive and the company of likeminded Christians—whatever view you have—is available, especially in the age of the Internet, relatively cheap telephone services, and so on. I do not mean, of course, that it is always and everywhere easy for people to think these things through. There are families, churches, and communities in which the consensus is so strong that anyone holding a deviant view—or even just considering an alternative—is under strong pressure, whether they're in a liberal situation in one place or a conservative situation in another. Still, however, most people can access resources to help them sort things through beyond merely what happens to "feel right" to them. And, again, because we finite and fallen human beings are so easily misled, we must not settle for easily gained answers to important and vexed questions when God puts other resources within our reach.

I want to make clear, however, that I am sympathetic to those women who, through the ages, have followed an inner voice into authentic Christian service. For, again, what else could God's Spirit in such extreme situations do to lead them to that service, if not give them a direct intuition? Realistically, there wasn't much to work with, given the overwhelming and reinforcing consensus in Scriptural interpretation, church teaching and practice, and societal patterns regarding patriarchy. So we do not have to condemn our sisters in the past for substandard theological methods. We can, instead, commend good theological method to our sisters (and brothers) today who want to make the best use of all of God's gifts in order to come to the best conclusions possible.

Let's move on, then, to discuss how we ought to make up our minds.

How I Changed My Mind

MOST OF THIS BOOK IS THEOLOGICAL ARGUMENT. But for people to change their minds on this complex and important issue is not merely a matter of following a valid argument to its end and saying, "Well, then. I'm convinced. That's that." Gender is such a fraught issue for many people that to change one's mind on it amounts to a kind of intellectual and ethical conversion experience. So let me now, as a good evangelical should, offer you a sort of conversion narrative.

I was raised in a Christian home—indeed, a *really* Christian home: a Plymouth Brethren home, with Brethren roots reaching back for several generations on both sides. Those who know about this small Protestant denomination know that people in its circles tend to be pretty serious about Christian faith: about Christian doctrine, about Christian morality, about Christian evangelism, and about other good things.

It was not only a Christian home; furthermore, it was also a Focus on the Family–type home. Dad was the full-time breadwinner (a surgeon) and Mom was the full-time homemaker (having quit school teaching to bear the first of four children—yours truly). Dad was an elder in our church who occasionally preached and taught Sunday school, while Mom was an exemplary "Mrs. Elder," helping the church ladies (as they called themselves then) run a myriad of service organizations and charities. She also took her turn playing the piano for worship services.

The Plymouth Brethren have a peculiar liturgical tradition that raised the question of gender for me from an early age. Typically, the Brethren celebrate communion at a special meeting early each Sunday morning. This "breaking of the bread" proceeds with virtually no fixed order of service except perhaps a formal greeting from a presiding elder and a subsequent closing, and with the passing of the bread and the cup sometime toward the end of the meeting. But aside from the welcome and the closing, anyone can rise in the silence and give out the number of a hymn, which the congregation then sings, or pray aloud, or even offer an exposition of Scripture. Some people prepare well in advance for their participation in the service; others jump up on the spur of an inspiration. The Brethren believe that the Holy Spirit guides the service quite directly, leading first one, then another, to participate—just as 1 Corinthians 14 indicates that the Spirit will. This free-form openness to the Holy Spirit's leadership amounts to a kind of charismatic worship—yet without any speaking in tongues, prophecies, healings, or other spectacular manifestations of the Spirit that would have caused consternation, not celebration, among the Brethren (who were scrupulously opposed to anything "pentecostal").

This kind of meeting—which I often found quite moving—raised the gender question in a fundamental respect. Anyone could lead in this service—not just clergy, for the Brethren have been unusual in generally having no such thing as ordination and therefore no formal clergy. And young people were encouraged to participate as freely as older ones. Anyone, I say, could lead—as long as that one was male.

Thus I sat in the family pew and observed various men participating week after week. Some did so with evident gifting and passion. But others seemed to do so by rote, with little attendant blessing reported by anyone else. And I began to wonder why my mother, who was otherwise so esteemed as a leader in our church, remained demurely silent week after week, and year after year, while Mr. So-and-so rose to bore us once again with his meanderings through Scripture, and Mr. Such-and-such followed with his interminable prayer. And when young Bill or even younger Bobby was encouraged to lead in the service while their mothers and grandmothers silently looked on, my wonder deepened.

Again, the point is that in most churches such questions don't arise quite so directly because such spiritual leading is reserved for clergy. The clergy/laity distinction predominates over the male/female one. But among the Brethren in this extraordinary service, where the former distinction wasn't operative, leadership was open to anyone— so long as he was male. Thus gender came to the fore.

In my later teens, I began to ask questions of my church's elders about gender. I received disappointing answers from very nice men clearly out of their depth. (One creatively affirmed, when pressed, that when the apostle Paul commanded women to have their heads covered when they prayed and prophesied, he meant "prayed silently" and "prophesied—in song.") I raised the same questions also at the Brethren Bible school I attended, and of the elders in the church I subsequently attended while at university. I received better answers, but they did not satisfy.

At the same time, I began to encounter more and more Christian women who seemed easily to be the spiritual equals of the men I had seen in church leadership: the sponsor of my high school Christian fellowship, Mrs. Krucker; my Aunt Jan, who during the year I boarded with my relatives while at Bible school taught me about the mysteries of women, dating, and marriage in the evenings at the kitchen table (while my Uncle Nelson taught me the New Testament during the days at school); two other wise and spiritual aunts, Donna-Jean and Valerie, whom I visited whenever I could during my undergraduate years; and the capable InterVarsity Christian Fellowship staff workers I met. I also met women among my fellow students who were obviously at least as mature, at least as wise, at least as gifted, and at least as pious as any of us young men. And radiant among these impressive women was Kari Sleeth, who became my wife, and whose first serious conversation with me was an extended midnight discussion about gender in the church and its apological implications. (Yes, it is of such magical moments that true romance is born.)

This was the late 1970s, so all of these developments in my life were happening within a broad social transformation of gender. People my age were seeing women enter all occupations, and we were learning to use new, generic titles for them: "police officers" and "firefighters" and "flight attendants." There was new talk of a "glass ceiling" that was keeping women from the very top positions in business and the professions, but the fact that it was recognized meant that the glass would shatter soon, as it did in many places. Society at large was making way for women everywhere, if sometimes grudgingly, and increasingly it was scandalous even to grumble about such changes, let alone resist them.

I'm a professional theologian, so let me resort to that discourse for a moment and say that by this point in my life, to echo Thomas Kuhn's helpful terminology in *The Structure of Scientific Revolutions*, the anomalies in my experience were accumulating at a rate too great to be accommodated by my paradigm.[1] And my mental situation was mirrored in my matrimonial one: Kari and I got married after I had completed my first degree, and I left for graduate school with an egalitarian marriage but without a thoroughly constructed theological basis for it. A master's program in theological studies at Wheaton College ensued, and then further training at the University of Chicago.

Finally, one afternoon, while studying in the tiny living room of our student apartment in Chicago while Kari was at work at the hospital across the street, I underwent an explosive paradigm shift. Yes, we come—already!—to the promised key to the lock, the clue to the puzzle, the Answer to the Problem.

I had been struggling with gender questions again, and had been reading on various sides of the issue. At the crucial moment I have described, I had been reading yet another explanation of 1 Timothy 2:11-15, easily one of the most obscure of the classic passages on this matter. And I remember quite clearly now—more than twenty years later—putting the book down on my lap and realizing this insight: nobody could explain this passage.

To be sure, I had been reading more than a dozen *attempts* to explain this passage. Some of them were ingenious; a few were even likely. But it struck me with paradigm-shaking force that no one could explain all of the clauses in this passage with full plausibility. And I then began to think that this problem was true not only of expositions of this one text, but of the whole gender question. No one I had read (and I had read quite a few) could put all of the relevant texts together into a single, finished puzzle with no pieces left over, no pieces manufactured to fill in gaps, and no pieces forced into place. I began to recall, with mounting excitement, how champions of one view typically ignored or explained away the leading texts of champions of other views. (This phenomenon is what lawyers call avoiding or finessing the "bad facts" of a case.)

So I came to a principle of general theological method out of this wrestling with the particular issue of gender: We should not wait to come to a theological conclusion for the happy day in which we have perfectly arranged all of the relevant texts. Instead, we should look at all of the texts as open-mindedly as possible, and see whether among the various competing interpretations there is one that makes the most sense of the most texts and especially the most important ones. We should look, in basic epistemological terms, for the preponderance of warrants or grounds to believe p instead of q. If no such preponderance is evident, of course, then we should suspend making a decision. But if we do conclude that a preponderance is discernible, then we should acknowledge it—indeed, be grateful for it—and proceed to act on that basis.

For what else can we do in theology? Jaroslav Pelikan, among many other historians of doctrine, has shown how the New Testament provides texts about the nature of the incarnation that can fairly be read as supporting various heresies (such as adoptionism, Arianism, modalism, and Nestorianism), while the church has concluded that the *best* reading of the *most* texts and the *most important* texts leads to the orthodox conclusions of the early church set out in the Chalcedonian Definition of 451.[2] Predestination and free will, faith and works, so-called charismatic phenomena, the nature of the end times—I am not persuaded that there is one and only one theological position on such controversies that provides the best interpretation of every single relevant text and then nicely packages them together in an effortlessly coherent whole.

So, I concluded, the theological task is not to be understood as "figuring it all out," so that one day a person or a church can finally say, "There, now! That's the answer!" with precision and certainty. If we can, indeed, validly come to clear and confident conclusions, all the better, of course. But the task fundamentally is to dwell on the Bible, with the help of the Holy Spirit and the church; to make the best decision one can make about what Scripture means; and then to respond to it in faith, obedience, and gratitude. Indeed, such a posture of interpretative humility entails remaining continually open to refinement of one's interpretations, and even to the acceptance of quite different positions as the Holy Spirit gives one more light. (I hope readers of this book will maintain that posture as you read, just in case the Holy Spirit offers something new to you as you do so.)[3]

In my reflections on the theological literature I had read, I went on to recognize that champions of various positions sometimes attacked each other's views—and often each other—on grounds other than theological. Feminists accused traditionalists of sexism: the traditionalists claimed to believe that women and men were equal, but they promptly relegated women to subservient positions in church and home—and society too, in the case of telling them to stay home and look after husband and children. (The really hard-line ones bragged that they would refuse a speeding ticket from a female police officer. I am not making this up.)[4] The traditionalists could never explain just why it was better for all women everywhere to remain in these domestic roles while all men everywhere were to be breadwinners out in the marketplace. Wasn't this scheme simply a baptized version of modern social sector differentiation, a phenomenon that emerged only in postagrarian industrial societies? This domestic arrangement was not in fact *traditional* at all—except in the historically shortsighted sense of "what Mom and Dad did back in the 1950s and '60s." So why should such roles be acclaimed as perennially normative?[5]

Furthermore, the feminists argued, there didn't seem to be anything essential to being a woman that would make her unfit for leadership in home, church, or society, and the traditionalists rarely suggested (anymore) that there was some inherent flaw of this sort. In the bad old days, women were derided as "emotional," "irrational," "illogical," "defensive," and the like, and therefore truly seemed unfit for important responsibilities.[6] Thus women were instead put in charge of children (!) and given other domestic jobs that, for men in the marketplace and in church leadership, were relatively uninteresting and unimportant. And that all made a kind of sense: if women couldn't handle leadership, then it was best that they weren't given any.[7]

Rarely, however, does one hear that sort of argument today. Instead, traditionalists typically praise women to the skies as fully equal to men. It's not that women are inferior, they say; it's just that God wants women not to lead in home and church (and possibly elsewhere), and we shouldn't disobey God. What has not been made clear in the current debate, feminists maintain, is just *why* God would want that, when he seems—by all accounts, on every side of this issue—to have made women evidently quite capable of leadership in all other spheres of society.[8] (Margaret Thatcher's career as British prime minister in the 1970s and 1980s loomed large as a case in point throughout the English-speaking world. Women as chief executives in businesses, universities, hospitals, and other institutions have multiplied the local and national examples.) God seems to have good reasons for his other commands; what is his good reason for this one?[9]

Among the most powerful arguments offered in turn by the complementarians was the charge of arrogance: Why did the feminists imply, if they didn't say outright, that the rest of the Christian church since the time of the apostles was wrong in regard to gender? Given the virtually unbroken tradition of patriarchy—male leadership and authority—with exceptions too few and too eccentric (if not heretical and schismatic) to take seriously, how dare the egalitarians suggest that they alone, and only today, teach the truth about the correct relations of men and women? Indeed, most of the global church today continues to organize itself in terms of male leadership. So the egalitarians are implicitly claiming that those Christians also are either mistaken on a basic point of Christian practice or are instead willfully perpetuating sinful structures of male domination and female oppression. In short, many complementarians say, the egalitarians claim that everyone else has been either too stupid or too sinful to see the light.

These accusations remind us that Christians do, and should, decide about things not only on the basis of Bible study, but also as we consult other sources as well: tradition, scholarship, experience, and more. Moreover, we properly consult these resources not on our own, but in the company of the church—the church of the past and the church of the present—seeking guidance from the Holy Spirit through all of these resources. Theology is the task of coordinating the deliverances of all of these gifts of God, and then formulating our best estimation of what God is saying to us, today, in this context, for his purposes in this moment.

It is deficient theology, therefore, that halts all deliberation with mere prooftexting ("The Bible says it; I believe it; that settles it"); or with appeals to current social practice ("Women lead businesses, universities, and governments—it's just ridiculous not to have them lead churches"); or with claims of personal intuition ("I just feel led to pastoral leadership"); or with any other shortcut. And it is disturbing how many churchgoers are content to settle for such simplistic methods that are so clearly vulnerable to manipulation by one's own or others' interests.

Likewise, many Christians affirm that it is arrogant theology that suggests that this or that formulation of doctrine or practice is a perfectly formulated and timeless truth for the ages that we must believe and obey without question. There is no "golden age," no point in the past at which a particular group of Christians in a particular place somehow managed to transcend time and space and their own peculiarities to think universal thoughts and set out transcultural absolutes for all subsequent Christian thought. Instead, we should revere the great creeds; we should honor the major catechisms and confessions; we should receive the liturgical, political, devotional, and other traditions of our forebears with appropriate respect, and gratitude. But we should also be careful not to confuse those treasures with the gospel itself, or with the supremely authoritative Bible, or with the ongoing guidance of the Holy Spirit of God in the current life of this part of the church. We must be open to hearing fresh words of God that help this part of the church cooperate with God in the work of his kingdom in its particular situation.

4

Two More Theological Clues

LET'S NOW CONSIDER TWO MORE methodological points that helped me move beyond my tense position of wanting to endorse the full participation of women in church and their truly equal status at home, while yet not seeing how I could justify such a move, given the biblical texts that seemed to forbid it.

The first principle of theological method of this remaining pair deals with what we might call "control texts." While we believe that all of the Bible is inspired by God, there are some texts of the Bible that clearly dominate our interpretation and reception of the others since those texts deal with more fundamental matters or provide summaries of other texts. Most obvious of such passages is Jesus' own epitome of the law in the two great commandments to love God with all one has and is, and to love one's neighbor as oneself. On these two texts, Jesus said, "hang all the law and the prophets" (Mt 22:40). Wise Christians recognize, then, that some parts of the Bible are more basic than others in any given discussion. But deciding which texts occupy which place in a hierarchy of control texts is not always easy.

In gender debates, egalitarians tend to use Galatians 3:28 as a text that governs everything else: "There is no longer Jew or Greek, there is no longer slave or free, there is no longer male and female; for all of you are one in Christ Jesus." Complementarians typically reply that this text should be more narrowly understood as applying to salvation, not to every aspect of life here and now. They point out, for example, that the difference between Jews and Greeks was acknowledged in the Great Council of Acts 15 and that the system of slavery was condoned by Paul in numerous writings in which he addresses slaves and masters (notably in the epistle to Philemon, but also in parallel passages dealing with household relations in Eph 6 and Col 3; cf. 1 Pet 2). So it doesn't make sense to assume that Galatians 3:28 means that no Christian distinction should properly remain between male and female.

For their part, many complementarians argue that whatever else may be ambiguous or controversial in the Bible about gender, it is clear that women are to keep quiet in church meetings: "As in all the churches of the saints, women should be silent in the churches. For they are not permitted to speak, but should be subordinate, as the law also says. If there is anything they desire to know, let them ask their husbands at home. For it is shameful for a woman to speak in church" (1 Cor 14:33-35; cf. 1 Tim 2:11-12).

Egalitarians respond that this interpretation of Paul's instructions seems a curious one, given that earlier in the very same epistle he has given instructions for women to cover their heads precisely when they "pray or prophesy." One might try to argue that the praying in view here is merely private prayer, but that seems very unlikely given that the theme of this section of the letter is corporate, not individual, worship. And prophecy intrinsically is a corporate activity: one hardly prophesies to oneself! So, egalitarians argue, Paul *cannot* have enjoined "silence" as the total absence of women's voices in public services—even if complementarians suggest that it is clear that that's what he meant.

Thus we recognize both the importance and the peril of discerning which texts are most fundamental, which texts properly "control" the interpretation of other texts, as we work at theology. In this regard, we do well to consider the importance of the so-called hermeneutical circle: the moving back and forth between what one assumes are control texts and what one assumes are secondary texts, seeing how well the data are explained by this relationship, with the possibility ever open that one not only might have to adjust one's interpretation of this or that text, but also might have to move texts from one category to another as one works toward the best arrangement of them all. Which verses do provide the normative context in which we can make the best sense of the others?

The hermeneutical circle—or, as some hopefully put it, the hermeneutical *spiral* that gets us closer and closer to the truth—shows up also in our last consideration in this chapter. In this version of the spiral, we recognize that when we investigate a matter, we are always moving back and forth between our *general* idea of what's going on and the *particular* bits of information that we have gathered from which we interpret what's going on. As we gather new bits or reinterpret bits we already have on hand, we might then confirm our general idea, or adjust it, or even replace it with a different general idea. Yet we also recognize that we always have a general idea of some sort that is governing our interpretation of the bits. In fact, if we didn't already have a general idea of what we're dealing with, we wouldn't know even what sorts of bits to look for, or what questions to ask of them, or what categories in which to place them, and so on.

Thus we have a dialectic, a back-and-forth motion between the parts and the whole. The general idea guides our looking for, and at, the bits, while our interpretation of the bits then feeds back into refining our general idea. And one of the important implications of this model of how we think about things is this final principle that we can, so to speak, enter the circle/spiral anywhere we like: at either the level of the general or the level of the particular.

Many Christians believe as simply an assumption (I used to do so) that the best way to proceed intellectually on any matter, and theologically in particular, is to enter the circle at the level of the particular. The responsible thinker, according to this model, gathers all the relevant bits together—from tradition, scholarship, experience, art, and especially the Bible—and then tries to discern what general pattern best explains them all. This way of proceeding is called *induction*. Too simple a view of this way of thinking, however, fails to acknowledge what we have just recognized: that from the very start we always have some general pattern in mind that guides our investigation. For example, we always assume certain criteria of relevance for selecting what are the "relevant bits," and those criteria come from the general idea with which we approach the investigation. We are never "just looking" at "the data."

Still, we don't need to abandon induction. Now more properly self-conscious of the role being played by our preconceptions, we proceed to gather our data. What else, in fact, can we do, but simply the best we can? Aware of our biases, however, we can try to be not *too* confident as we induce a general idea from our investigation, and we will remain humbly open to alternative views. We realize that we might have missed something important because our general idea did not incline us to look for it in the first place or to take it seriously if we happened upon it. And we recognize that we can never know that we have discovered all of the relevant data—an inherent limitation in all induction.

However intuitively obvious it may be to many of us that rigorous thinking proceeds inductively, and therefore that theology proceeds from just reading the Bible bit by bit and seeing what comes out of it (!), it is important to see that we can legitimately proceed a different way: by beginning instead at the level of the general theory, or *hypothesis*. We first acknowledge, as we have seen, that we all do have such preconceptions—and perhaps we might already have deliberately devised a fairly elaborate theory. Having such preconceptions is unavoidable, and intentionally constructing a possible interpretation (based on previous encounters with relevant data) is perfectly acceptable so long as one then submits it to rigorous testing against all the data one can find. In fact, it is crucial to test one's hypothesis against not only all the data one can find oneself, but also against all the data and all the countervailing arguments offered by opponents of one's theory. Only if the theory stands up well against these tests can one enjoy reasonable confidence in it.

We do well to consider other possible outcomes of this testing, of course. If one's theory fails to explain *some* data as well as a competing theory does, one still is justified in maintaining allegiance to one's theory if the competing theory does not, *overall*, do a better job of explaining all of the relevant data and responding to all counter-arguments. The quest is not for the *perfect* theory, the perfect interpretation of Scripture, the perfect theology. For who do we think we are? As limited human beings, we properly must settle for what *seems* to be the *best* of the *available* interpretations.

To be sure, if one's theory doesn't do a satisfactory job and no alternative looks any better, then the responsible choice is to suspend one's allegiance to *any* theory, pending more data or better arguments. Sometimes the best decision is *not* to decide just yet. (In fact, that was my own considered opinion for a number of years: a well-informed "I don't know.")

Still, the theological quest is properly understood as seeking the *best* ideas *we* can find in *these* circumstances. Furthermore, we must always remember that the main goal of life is not to figure everything out, but to do God's will. We thus rely on God to provide for us what we need to accomplish his will in every circumstance, including the best theology for the job—and to then get on with that work.[1] So we don't even have to *aspire* to perfect theology, but to theology that is adequate and appropriate to getting done what God wants done among us here and now. If we insist on waiting for a perfect theory that explains everything properly and easily, we will delay while work languishes, people suffer, and God shakes his head. The brightest minds in physics and philosophy, art and architecture, medicine and mothering don't wait until they have everything figured out. Why should theologians?

ONWARD TO THE ARGUMENT

With these considerations in mind, then, here is how I would like to proceed. I was taught to think the inductive way as a Christian—and in this case that would mean working through Bible texts one by one, then going on to the history of theology and of the church's gender practices, and finally perhaps trying to sort all of this out in the light of contemporary gender studies and social experiences. But it will be more efficient for us both if I work from the other side of the hermeneutical circle.

In the next chapter, therefore, I will set out a theory I have already constructed: a model for understanding gender. It is a model based on even more fundamental Christian considerations, such as the nature of the church, the mission of God in the world, the characteristic way the Holy Spirit fulfills that mission, and so on. (It will become clear that many of the control verses I think make a significant difference regarding gender focus most directly on other issues, but their implications are crucial for deciding about the matters before us.) I will proceed to explain some of the implications of this theory for the Christian home and church, as well as for society at large. And I will offer arguments supporting this theory from the Bible, from the history of the church, and from contemporary reason and experience. Finally, I will test this theory by posing against it the objections of countertheories, and particularly the best arguments of the complementarians.

Am I a completely objective adjudicator of these various competing theories, and thus capable of rendering an infallible and universally valid judgment? Of course not. Obviously, I am nowhere near the Enlightenment ideal of utter, disinterested objectivity. But then, to put it gently, neither are you. We cannot escape our limitations and imperfections, our interests and our agendas. Nor can we evade, or even indefinitely defer, our responsibility to make up our minds and live as obediently as we can in the light of what we perceive to be God's word. So let me introduce the understanding of gender that replaced my traditional one, and let's just do our best to see how well it works.

5

The Model

AS ONE READS THE RECENT CHRISTIAN literature on gender, it
is impressive how confident so many authors seem to be about the
correctness of their position and the patent error of their opponents'.
No one quite says this explicitly, but the implication is clear: "My
position *is* obviously the right position, and all who differ with me are
therefore simply wrong. They are badly confused, if they are not in
fact *evil*, in resisting the pellucid truth of what I'm saying."

Let me say immediately that I agree that there are indeed some
fundamental Christian affirmations that ought to be affirmed by any
faithful Christian as basic and clear. A Christian must affirm that
"Jesus is Lord," or one just is not a Christian in any spiritually important sense. Christianity properly condemns pride, lust, greed, and
the other deadly sins. "All have sinned and come short of the glory of
God"; "God was in Christ reconciling the world to himself"; "You
must be born again"; "I am the way, the truth, and the life; no one
comes to the Father except through me." Contrary to the assertion by
some theologians, including orthodox ones, that theology must
always speak analogically, I think these statements, and many others,
are univocally true—that is, just plain true.

It is evident, however, that the Bible offers more complicated
wisdom on quite a number of matters. In some cases, what was once
allowed is now condemned: for example, divorce by a simple writ by
a dissatisfied husband (Mt 5:31-32). In some cases, what was once

commanded is now done away with as otiose: for example, the entire Old Testament sacrificial system, as interpreted in the epistle to the Hebrews. In some cases, what is mandated for some is not mandated for others: for example, adherence to the Jewish law by Jewish Christians but not by Gentile Christians (Acts 15:23-29). In some cases, what is troubling to some is declared to be actually of no consequence—*unless* such a thing would trouble one's conscience *or* cause another Christian confusedly to stumble back into sinful ways, in which case it is indeed important; the same example paradoxically serves for both principles, namely, eating meat offered to idols (1 Cor 8; cf. 1 Cor 10:25-30; Rom 14:14-23). The Bible's teaching is often complex, subtle, and even ambiguous—for the trained interpreter as well as for the ordinary reader.

I did not want to think that the Bible was hard to understand about gender, however. I wanted to think simply and clearly about it. In particular, I wanted to be a feminist all the way (back before *feminist* became the "f-word" that no decent person would use in public). I believed in women and men as coequal partners before God, bearers together of God's image, with no job or role or responsibility closed to either of them except where sheer biology dictated that only one sex could bear children. This simple position made the most sense of the world around me, made the most sense of my experiences of capable women both within and outside the church, and made the most sense of my relationship with my wife. But an egalitarian position did *not* make the most sense of the tradition of the church, and neither did it square with a number of Bible verses that seemed forthrightly to forbid a woman from exercising coequal leadership in the family or the congregation.

Now, let me pause to recognize again that I am deliberately oversimplifying the situation in what follows. There are not simply two positions on gender among evangelicals, but several. For example, some evangelicals have allowed women to preach, but only in foreign missionary situations (what I call "the missionary exception"). Others allow women to participate in spiritual leadership, but only in so-called parachurch organizations, and not in congregations and denominations (what I call "the parachurch parenthesis"). And still others permit women to have even wide-ranging theological careers of speaking and writing, as long as they profess to be responsible to a man, whether husband or pastor or both (the "under authority arrangement"). Many of us, however, do not want to settle for any of these intermediate models, but prefer to consider a full-blown egalitarianism. So the either/or of egalitarianism and complementarianism are the terms of the following discussion as well.[1]

I propose, then, a paradigm of gender that does, indeed, draw no lines between men and women as to role in home, church, or society—beyond those required by biology. Unlike many egalitarians, however, I will do so in large part by listening to the views of my complementarian counterparts. They simply are not wrong about everything. Furthermore, I believe that the typical egalitarian argumentation (particularly the so-called redemptive movement hermeneutic) can and must be improved on as well.[2]

Having set out my defense of egalitarianism, I will then qualify this radical position. And I will do so in some ways so drastic that, as I acknowledge here up front, many egalitarians will reject it as in fact betraying the cause of feminism. Yet this model of understanding gender seems to me to make the most sense of most of the most important data, and a number of smaller details as well. So I hold to it—until a better paradigm comes into view.

6

Equality

THE FIRST PRINCIPLE OF THIS MODEL is that men and women are equal in dignity before God. Genesis 1 records the human person as being created in God's image, and as created male and female in that image (Gen 1:26-27). The creation mandate to procreate so as to co-create the world with God is given to man and woman as the partnership they are—the humans—without any sense that one is somehow lesser or inferior.

The second, and different, creation story of Genesis 2 shows the human being divided by God into male and female individuals. We can note that the self-consciousness of the previously undivided human "goes with" the male, and it is he who then recognizes and celebrates the female as his partner upon their differentiation. But the passage carries on into a celebration of marriage: the two human beings (re-)join together as they separate from their birth families, literally re-forming the originally undivided human (Gen 2:18-24). I cannot imagine a stronger set of images of coequality, partnership and the like.

Then as we pass over, for now, the fall in Genesis 3 and the subsequent history of redemption recounted in the Old Testament, we encounter Jesus befriending and teaching women—sometimes to the scandal of onlookers, given the strict separation of the sexes in public—and women caring for him in return. Among numerous examples, the most prominent perhaps are the Samaritan woman (Jn 3), Mary Magdalene (Mk 15:40-41; Lk 8:1-3), and Mary and Martha (Lk

10:38-42; Jn 11:1-44; 12:1-8). Indeed, he calls Mary Magdalene to be the "first Christian," the first one to recognize him as having risen from the dead and the first one to herald that good news to others.[1] Jesus repeatedly trespasses across the gender lines of his culture to affirm, serve, and enjoy women as he also delights in men.

We next encounter the Holy Spirit being poured out on women and men together as the prophecy of Joel is invoked to explain the spectacle of Pentecost (Acts 2:16-18). We encounter Galatians 3:28 and the declaration that in Christ all of the barriers that divide people from each other into "better" and "worse," "insiders" and "outsiders," are removed: no more first-class versus second-class citizens in the kingdom of Christ. No Jew feeling more holy than the mere Gentile; no male lording it over the female; no free person exploiting a slave. We encounter lists of spiritual gifts and church functions that never are categorized as "for men only," "for women only," and "for both" (e.g., Rom 12:6-8; 1 Cor 12:8-10, 27-30; Eph 4:11). And we also encounter Paul sending commendatory words about women playing various roles in the churches to which he writes—including women identified as coworker, "deacon," and even "apostle" (Rom 16:1-12).

There are lots of scriptural clues, therefore, to indicate that the egalitarians are right: God originally intended women and men to be coequal partners in stewarding the earth, without one being subordinate to the other, and God has never rescinded that mandate. Indeed, in God's renewal of all things, in his great salvation plan to restore shalom, men and women will treat each other as they were intended to treat each other—and we already see this renewed order in the inbreaking of the kingdom evident in the New Testament.

Yet egalitarians often fail to listen to their complementarian brothers and sisters who point out several cogent objections, or at least qualifications, to this vision. Let's listen to those concerns.

First, the testimony of most of the Bible—from Genesis 3 until the last epistles of the New Testament—bespeaks an overwhelming pattern of patriarchy. Men are in charge, and they are supposed to be in charge, for almost all of the Bible.

Second, God depicts his own relationship with Israel, and then Christ's with the church, in terms of a patriarchal marriage of nonequals. God/Christ is the superior power, the initiator and sustainer of the relationship, the leader and the provider—and Israel/church is the grateful respondent.[2]

Third, Jesus did indeed welcome women into his circle of disciples—but not his inner circle. That was reserved for the Twelve, not one of whom was a woman. Many scholars argue that the Twelve are symbolic of the new Israel that Jesus is constituting in his ministry, so the selection of twelve free Jewish males coheres with that symbolism. Egalitarians simply have to recognize that Jesus did not select Jewish women, or Gentiles, or slaves. One might wonder— even as a complementarian—why there was so much symbolic continuity with the distinctions of class, ethnicity, and sex typical of the old covenant if the new Israel is to completely do away with all such distinctions. And, to be sure, the Twelve are a first generation–only class that gives way after their deaths to the roles of elders, teachers, prophets, and other leaders—some of whom, egalitarians rush to point out, seem to have been women. But the point remains, as we all must recognize, that Jesus "transgresses" only so far in his public life—to the point of occasional scandal, yes, but not of anything approaching gender revolution.

For his part, Paul does recognize and affirm women's service to the church. But he also expressly forbids (at least some) women to teach or have authority over (at least some) men (at least sometimes). Indeed, women apparently are to keep silent in church services (1 Cor 14:33-35; cf. 1 Tim 2:11-12). So whatever else women do—and complementarians insist that women are invaluable and active members of churches then and now—Paul seems to teach that they are not to lead.

So I would like to suggest a way to understand gender that pays respect to both sides. I would like to offer a way that avoids simply ruling out the contentions of either side, since I find valid points in each and, perhaps more significantly, since I find exemplary Christians advocating both positions. (Again, the only alternative is to conclude that all of those holy and intelligent people who disagree with me are just flat wrong—and why think that unlikely thought if one does not need to do so?) In particular, I would like to find a way to keep from suggesting that the Bible contradicts itself, and particularly to avoid the intolerable conclusion that Jesus and Paul contradict themselves.[3]

To do so, I need to outline a set of principles that, taken together, both justify and qualify Christian egalitarianism in home, church, and society.

Gospel Priorities and Holy Pragmatism

IF EQUALITY IS THE FIRST PRINCIPLE IN this paradigm I am offering, the second principle is that since some things matter more than others, lesser things sometimes must be sacrificed in the interest of the greater. What matters most to God, it seems, is the furtherance of the gospel message. In the New Testament, and in subsequent church history, we see that God is willing to do almost anything to get the gospel out to as many people as possible, as effectively as possible. He then wants this message to take root and bear as much fruit as possible. The New Testament indicates also that God expects his people to participate in what we might call this holy pragmatism.[1]

We might wonder why God Almighty doesn't just accomplish all of his purposes entirely and at once. Why must there be any such tradeoff? But we are now asking the age-old question of the nature of God's providence, within which lie such profound matters as the problem of evil, the "delay" of Christ's return, and so on. Clearly, we cannot set out a full-blown doctrine of providence here, but we must bear in mind that God's providence has a different timetable than we might ourselves prefer. His ways are higher than our ways, and his thoughts than our thoughts (Is 55:9). We also must appreciate that God can do anything God wants to do, but also *only what can be done*. If there is no easier way to do something, then God must do it the hard way—as Jesus acknowledged in the Garden of Gethsemane.[2]

We encounter now, therefore, the principle of *accommodation*. God works within human limitations—both individual and corporate limitations—to transform the world according to his good purposes. To be blunt, God works with what he's got—and with what we've got. When faced with our shortcomings and sin, God doesn't just erase us and create a whole new situation. Instead, God graciously pursues shalom in the glory and the mess that we have made. The living water of the Holy Spirit very rarely comes like a tsunami, forcing everything it encounters to submit to its will. Instead, God's Spirit graciously, humbly, and wisely pours over the extant topography of the social landscape, conforming himself to the contours he encounters. As he does so, however, like an irresistible flow of water he reshapes the landscape by and by, eventually making the crooked ways straight and the rough places plain (Is 40:3-4).[3]

William Webb offers a helpful summary of reasons why God might act in the gradual, accommodating way he has regarding patriarchy.

> *Pastoral:* to "stretch" the covenant people as far as they could go (like an elastic band), but not wanting them to "snap." Change is always difficult. God brings his people along in ways that were feasible adaptations. *Pedagogical:* to take people from where they are (the known) and help them move to a foreseeable future (the unknown) that has enough continuity with the present so that they can find their way into the preferred future. *Evangelistic:* to make the Christian lifestyle evangelistically winsome to unbelievers. The reform was enough to better existing sociological structures, but not so radical that it would jeopardize other aspects of Christian mission or overtly threaten governmental structures. *Competing values:* to sustain other good values at least temporarily within a less redemptive framework. . . . *Soteriological:* to deal with humanity's sinful and stubborn condition. Reform does not come easily to a dark side within fallen humanity. God's revelation took measured steps (not unrealistic leaps) in the progressive sanctification of social structures.[4]

In the same pattern of divine behavior, therefore, we encounter the apparent scandal of Jesus not healing everyone, or delivering everyone from captivity, or raising everyone from the dead. Since Christians believe in God's loving and wise providence, we therefore believe that it was somehow more strategic for Jesus to limit his array of miracles—primarily to be signs pointing to the much more important phenomenon of the inbreaking of the kingdom through him. The miracles in themselves were wonderful, to be sure, but the wonder was to be directed then to the even more crucial matter of Jesus' authority and identity. Christians trust that God limits the good that he does in any given situation, and even allows evils to continue for a while, in order to accomplish the greater good of his ultimate purposes.

In just this way, I suggest, Jesus puts critical and creative pressure against the gender distinction of his culture—the way he also does against the Jew/Gentile distinction, against the Jew/Samaritan distinction, against the adult/child distinction, against the rich/poor distinction, and so on—but without going so far as to actually overturn it. Jesus treats patriarchy the way he treats so much else of the law and custom of his time: ambiguously, suggestively, and sometimes subversively, but never immediately, never revolutionarily, except when it comes to the central matter of his own mission and person. On that score, he provokes people literally to fling themselves at his feet in worship or to take up stones to kill him. Jesus puts first things first: the gospel of the kingdom of God, the message of eternal life, brought near in himself. The main scandal of Jesus' career is properly *Jesus*—not Jesus and feminism, or Jesus and the abolition of slavery, or Jesus and Jewish emancipation, or anything else. Those other causes are good, and I believe that they all are implicit in Jesus' ministry. But they are incipient at best, and the pattern of Jesus' accommodation to these various social distinctions while also putting them under serious pressure needs to be acknowledged and then accounted for in one's paradigm regarding gender. It therefore is obvious that I am disagreeing with those of my feminist friends who try to read egalitarianism directly out of the career of Jesus. I don't think one can do so: Jesus is not *that* revolutionary.

This is the basic pattern of God's activity: God gives all he has, and does all he can, within the situation he has sovereignly allowed to develop. He constantly sacrifices good things for better. Indeed, he "did not withhold his own Son" (Rom 8:32), but gave his life in order to secure the greater good of global redemption. And he expects us to make up "what is lacking in Christ's afflictions" (Col 1:24): to work, and to suffer, and even to die alongside him—indeed, to take up our crosses in daily acknowledgment that we are both his children and his slaves, as the apostles designate themselves, in order to achieve God's main objectives in our own lives and in the lives of others.

We would not need to concern ourselves with this matter of gospel priorities if the kingdom had indeed fully come two thousand years ago. And we will not need to rank them in the New Jerusalem, for shalom will have blossomed forth on every hand. As Christ showed Julian of Norwich, "All will be well, and all will be well, and all manner of thing will be well."[5] *Of course* the abolition of slavery is a high kingdom value. *Of course* ethnic distinctions are to be celebrated as manifestations of creative diversity and not to serve as grounds for hatred and oppression. *Of course* men are not to domineer over women nor women cower before, or kowtow to, men. These corruptions of God's good order are all destined for judgment and will disappear in the world to come.

You and I live now, however, in "the meanwhile." It is a commonplace of New Testament scholarship regarding the kingdom of God that it has come "already, but not yet": God's direct and glorious rule is already and authentically here, in and through Jesus Christ, but it is not yet fully realized in this world still deeply and broadly marred by sin. To help us make sense of our situation, let's look not only backward to Jesus and the Bible, but forward to the age to come. We need a third principle, one not always accounted for properly in discussions of gender: eschatology.

8

Eschatology

EGALITARIANS OFTEN ACCUSE complementarians of failing to recognize the inbreaking of the kingdom of God in the career of Jesus and in the bestowing of the Holy Spirit at Pentecost. Complementarians, it is alleged, fail to take eschatology seriously—particularly the declaration that the "last days" have arrived, per Peter's sermon in Acts 2. "You're living in the past," egalitarians say, "still living under the effects of the fall and thus perpetuating the male domination described in Genesis 3. You don't realize that we are now in a new era, the era of the last days, when patriarchy, along with other traditional compromises of God's good will, is to be done away with."

Yet egalitarians themselves are open to an opposite charge from the complementarian side—namely, that they are practicing a "realized eschatology" (some would say an *over*-realized eschatology): an eschatology that acts as if the end times have indeed *fully* come, and that we are to experience all of the blessings of the kingdom here and now. If there is too little "already" in the complementarian position, there is not enough "not yet" in most egalitarian teaching.

What would our understanding of gender look like, however, if we took the "already, but not yet" principle seriously? What if we were to expect, instead of one extreme or the other, an appropriately paradoxical situation: a slow and partial realization of gospel values here and there, as God patiently and carefully works his mysterious ways along the multiple fronts of kingdom advance?

The New Testament writers and audiences seem to expect the Lord's return at any time—and particularly within the lifetimes of some of the first readers. Indeed, Paul has to counsel the Thessalonians that the Lord has not returned already, but is expected soon (1 Thess 4:13–5:3). So it would make sense—given gospel priorities, holy pragmatism, and eschatological expectations—for the apostles to teach a policy of cultural conservatism ("Get along as best you can with the political powers and social structures that be") in the interest of accomplishing the one crucial task: spreading the gospel as far and as fast as possible. And they do.[1]

This outlook is so foreign to that of most modern Christians—although many Pentecostals and charismatics around the world do share such a lively belief in the imminence of the second coming—and yet so important for understanding our subject that it is worth considering several key passages in this regard. Let's look at three from Paul and one from Peter:

> But we urge you, beloved, . . . to aspire to live quietly, to mind your own affairs, and to work with your hands, as we directed you, so that you may behave properly toward outsiders and be dependent on no one. (1 Thess 4:10-12)

> If it is possible, so far as it depends on you, live peaceably with all. Beloved, never avenge yourselves, but leave room for the wrath of God; for it is written, "Vengeance is mine, I will repay, says the Lord." No, "if your enemies are hungry, feed them; if they are thirsty, give them something to drink; for by doing this you will heap burning coals on their heads." Do not be overcome by evil, but overcome evil with good.
>
> Let every person be subject to the governing authorities; for there is no authority except from God, and those authorities that exist have been instituted by God. Therefore whoever resists authority resists what God has appointed, and those who resist will incur judgment. For rulers are not a terror to good conduct, but to bad. Do you wish to have no fear of the authority? Then do what is good, and you will receive its approval; for it is God's servant for your good. But if you do

what is wrong, you should be afraid, for the authority does not bear the sword in vain! It is the servant of God to execute wrath on the wrongdoer. Therefore one must be subject, not only because of wrath but also because of conscience. For the same reason you also pay taxes, for the authorities are God's servants, busy with this very thing. Pay to all what is due them—taxes to whom taxes are due, revenue to whom revenue is due, respect to whom respect is due, honor to whom honor is due.

Owe no one anything, except to love one another; for the one who loves another has fulfilled the law. The commandments, "You shall not commit adultery; You shall not murder; You shall not steal; You shall not covet"; and any other commandment, are summed up in this word, "Love your neighbor as yourself." Love does no wrong to a neighbor; therefore, love is the fulfilling of the law.

Besides this, you know what time it is, how it is now the moment for you to wake from sleep. For salvation is nearer to us now than when we became believers; the night is far gone, the day is near. (Rom 12:18–13:12)

Let each of you remain in the condition in which you were called. Were you a slave when called? Do not be concerned about it. Even if you can gain your freedom, make use of your present condition now more than ever. For whoever was called in the Lord as a slave is a freed person belonging to the Lord, just as whoever was free when called is a slave of Christ. You were bought with a price; do not become slaves of human masters. In whatever condition you were called, brothers and sisters, there remain with God. . . . For the present form of this world is passing away. (1 Cor 7:20-24, 31; cf. 1 Tim 6:1; Tit 2:9-10)[2]

Conduct yourselves honorably among the Gentiles, so that, though they malign you as evildoers, they may see your honorable deeds and glorify God when he comes to judge.

For the Lord's sake accept the authority of every human institution, whether of the emperor as supreme, or of governors, as sent by him to punish those who do wrong and to praise those who do right. For it is God's will that by doing right you should silence the ignorance of the foolish. As servants of God, live as free people, yet do not use your freedom as a pretext for evil. Honor everyone. Love the family of believers. Fear God. Honor the emperor. (1 Pet 2:12-17)

Missionaries of every era and locale often have practiced exactly this policy. There was no point, in their circumstances, to undertaking a quixotic crusade against some deeply entrenched social evil when the church was tiny and young. Any such irritation (one could hardly call it a threat) to the powers would have been crushed in its cradle. And if you have transformation of society in mind, as Christians do who see now that Christ did not return in the first century and might not return for another twenty, then it is better to play the long game: to grow the church and then permeate society with gospel values, with the hope of eventually ameliorating or even transforming what was wrong.[3]

Yet even with this pragmatic accommodation to social realities for the sake of the gospel, we would also expect to see evidence of the kingdom "already" here: in the early church, and in every church. At least within Christian homes and churches—those institutions over which Christians would have the most immediate and extensive control—one would expect to see kingdom values at work: overcoming oppression, eliminating inequality, sharing resources, binding disparate people together in love and mutual respect, liberating gifts, and the like. We would expect to hear teaching that envisioned that great day when all such barriers to human fellowship are removed and everyone can fully flourish together. We would expect, in short, to catch glimpses of the kingdom and to feel its unstoppable momentum toward universal shalom, even while we also appreciate the way the Holy Spirit skillfully and patiently guides the church to make the most of whatever opportunities it has in this or that situation. And in many homes and churches, past and present, I think we do find exactly that sort of evidence of God's "kingdom come"—not as disobedient departures from God's commandment of perpetual patriarchy, but as faithful enjoyment of the life of the world to come, insofar as it can be enjoyed under the present regime. We shall examine examples of such enjoyment presently, in church history and even in the New Testament itself. Before we do, however, we also need to consider yet another paradoxical principle: the Christian liberty to give up precisely some of the freedoms won for us in Christ—again, for the sake of a higher good.

9

Liberty

THE APOSTLE PAUL GIVES US PARADOXICAL wisdom on "making the most of the time" in his teaching on Christian liberty (Eph 5:16; cf. Col 4:5). First, he asserts a radical freedom in Christ—freedom from law, freedom from social divisions, freedom from religious tradition, freedom even from the world, the flesh, and the devil. Paul's language can hardly be excelled in its breathtaking scope:

> If, because of the one man's trespass, death exercised dominion through that one, much more surely will those who receive the abundance of grace and the free gift of righteousness exercise dominion in life through the one man, Jesus Christ. . . . For the wages of sin is death, but the free gift of God is eternal life in Christ Jesus our Lord. . . . For the law of the Spirit of life in Christ Jesus has set you free from the law of sin and of death. (Rom 5:17; 6:23; 8:2)

> Grace to you and peace from God our Father and the Lord Jesus Christ, who gave himself for our sins to set us free from the present evil age, according to the will of our God and Father, to whom be the glory forever and ever. Amen. (Gal 1:3-5)

> For in Christ Jesus you are all children of God through faith. As many of you as were baptized into Christ have clothed yourselves with Christ. There is no longer Jew or Greek, there is no longer slave or free, there is no longer male and female; for all of you are one in Christ Jesus. (Gal 3:26-28)

Paul's teaching is echoed in the epistle to the Hebrews:

> Since, therefore, the children share flesh and blood, he himself likewise shared the same things, so that through death he might destroy the one who has the power of death, that is, the devil, and free those who all their lives were held in slavery by the fear of death. (Heb 2:14-15)

Inspired by the same Spirit who opens up this great theme of freedom, Paul locates this freedom in the world as it is now. And he counsels the prudent use of this freedom toward God's number-one priority: the drawing of women and men to himself, and upward to maturity, as the center of God's plan for global redemption. Thus Paul teaches the use of Christian liberty in a startling, even confounding, sense: the freedom *not* to enjoy freedom in this or that respect if such curtailment of liberty would promote the greater good.

> For you were called to freedom, brothers and sisters; only do not use your freedom as an opportunity for self-indulgence, but through love become slaves to one another. For the whole law is summed up in a single commandment, "You shall love your neighbor as yourself." (Gal 5:13-14)

> But when you thus sin against members of your family, and wound their conscience when it is weak, you sin against Christ. Therefore, if food is a cause of their falling, I will never eat meat, so that I may not cause one of them to fall. (1 Cor 8:12-13)

> "All things are lawful," but not all things are beneficial. "All things are lawful," but not all things build up. Do not seek your own advantage, but that of the other. (1 Cor 10:23-24; cf. 1 Pet 2:16)

Let's be clear that the actions in question are not sinful. If they were, they would simply be forbidden. In fact, Paul's point is that they are generally legitimate in themselves, but they become illegitimate if enjoying them will somehow impede the supreme cause of the spread of the gospel and the edification of the Christian community. Good things, then, are to be foregone in the interest of better things—and particularly in the interests of benefiting others, rather than oneself.[1]

To turn to our own subject, in many situations it would seem best for everyone involved for women to seize the opportunity to be free and whole and fully functioning, not trammeled and reduced by patriarchy. In fact, I maintain that that is exactly the situation in much of the world today. We all will benefit from the full emancipation and participation of women, and so we all should strive for it. But in many other cases throughout history, and even in some places in our world today, the social disruption of full-fledged feminism would come at too high a price. Disturbed families, churches, and societies might become more hostile toward the Christian religion—and likely with little or no actual gain in freedom for women. So this difficult and unattractive possibility of using one's liberty to freely constrain oneself continues to confront us.

In this teaching, Paul has in mind the supreme example of Christ:

Do nothing from selfish ambition or conceit, but in humility regard others as better than yourselves. Let each of you look not to your own interests, but to the interests of others. Let the same mind be in you that was in Christ Jesus,

who, though he was in the form of God,
  did not regard equality with God
  as something to be exploited,
but emptied himself,
  taking the form of a slave,
  being born in human likeness.
And being found in human form,
  he humbled himself
  and became obedient to the point of death—
  even death on a cross. (Phil 2:3-8)

Egalitarians properly rejoice in the liberty from oppression and particularly from patriarchy that is won for us in Christ. Freedom from gender discrimination is an important implication of the gospel. Yet this particular liberty, among many others, must at least sometimes be foregone in the greater liberty given us to do whatever is necessary to further the most fundamental message of the gospel: deliverance from sin and death, and reconciliation to God and the enjoyment of eternal life through knowing Jesus Christ our Lord.

I say this because for the Christian individual and the Christian church, the question of gender is not just about gender. It isn't even primarily about gender. It is about the kingdom of God—because *everything* is first and finally about the kingdom of God. And because everything is about the kingdom of God, then questions about gender need to be asked in this one, primary context: What will best advance the kingdom of God, here and now?[2]

10

Gift, Calling, Order, and Edification

LET'S TURN, AS PROMISED, TO THE New Testament's teaching about those crucial spheres of home and church. We find here four intertwining principles: gift, calling, order, and edification.

Paul gives us the most instruction on these matters, so we begin with his most extensive passage, 1 Corinthians 11–14. Paul here is concerned with the proper balancing of Christian values. He is delighted that the Corinthians want to participate in the life of the church, but he wants them to do so according to their genuine ability to do so. Thus he teaches that each Christian is gifted by the Holy Spirit, and we should then discern in what respect we are gifted and go on to play our appropriate role in the body of Christ. Indeed, God calls each of us to one or another role at this or that time. "Vocation" is not just for clergy, but for everyone.

Paul proceeds to explain that Christians best obey God's call and use their gifts when there is appropriate order in the church. Cacophony might be exciting, but there is no way for one Christian to help another—Paul uses the expression "build up" or "edify" another—in the canceling out of each other in all this noise. So Paul simply asks that people let each other serve in turn, according to their gifts. And he forbids the nonsense and chaos that stem from a selfish desire to enjoy one's own spirituality regardless of the benefit it might or might not bring to the other members of the church.

So do we see egalitarianism here or not? No, we don't—at least, not in the radical sense of "no differentiation of roles such that some exercise authority over others." It is abundantly clear, in fact, that there remains a wide range of hierarchies in the church and home in the pages of the New Testament. The complementarians are simply right about that:

- elders rule the church, and others follow (Acts 15; 1 Tim 5:17; 1 Pet 5:1-5);

- masters in the home give the orders, and slaves comply (Eph 6:5-9; Col 3:22-25; 1 Tim 6:1-2; Tit 2:9-10; 1 Pet 2:18);

- parents instruct, and children obey (Eph 6:1-4; Col 3:20-21; 1 Tim 3:4-5, 12); and

- men teach and exercise authority in the church, while women do not, and husbands are the heads of their wives, while their wives submit to them (1 Cor 14:34-35; 1 Tim 2:11-12; 1 Cor 11:1-10; Eph 5:22-33; Col 3:18-19; 1 Pet 3:1-7).

I realize that considerable effort has been expended by biblical feminists to explain one or another of these texts in a way that does not entail patriarchy. And perhaps in some cases such explanations are correct. Taken as a whole, however, the pattern of hierarchy seems evident. It seems to me to be a more hopeful theological strategy to look for a different way of understanding this pattern as a whole than to try to chip away at it one verse at a time.

We find, in fact, that these hierarchies include at least some that God cannot possibly mean to remain permanent. And that obvious impermanency is a clue to how we are to understand this general pattern in a way conducive to gender egalitarianism. Let's take the church situation first, and then we'll examine the domestic sphere.

THE CHURCH

I suggest that Paul means just what he says about gender. But I make this suggestion in a radical way: I think he means *everything* he says about gender, not just the favorite passages cited by one side or another. The fascinating question here is this: How can Paul sound so egalitarian sometimes and so complementarian—even simply patriarchal—at other times?

I suggest that Paul is guided by the Holy Spirit—even used by the Holy Spirit perhaps without his full awareness of the implications—to do two good things simultaneously: (1) to give the church prudent instruction as to how to survive and thrive in a patriarchal culture that he thinks won't last long; *and also* (2) to maintain and promote the egalitarian teaching that is evident throughout the Bible and dynamic particularly in the career of Jesus and that in the right circumstances will leave gender lines behind. This "doubleness" in Paul—which I aver we can see also in the ministry of Jesus, as well as in some key instances in the Old Testament, as we will note shortly—helps to explain one of the crucial facts of this debate: why egalitarians and complementarians both find support for their views herein.

Paul seems to believe that women should keep silence in church *and* that they should pray and prophesy. And this apparent contradiction appears in passages occurring in the very same letter, 1 Corinthians. How could women possibly obey him in both respects? By being silent at the right times, and praying and prophesying at the right times.

Paul prescribes silence for women in regard to corporate worship: "When you come together, each one has a hymn, a lesson, a revelation, a tongue, or an interpretation. Let all things be done for building up" (1 Cor 14:26). Women in this culture, as in most cultures in the history of the world, generally were not educated beyond the domestic arts. Furthermore, they were not socialized into the discourse of formal, public learning. So in the enthusiasm of their Christian liberty, in the excitement of the freedom found in their full acceptance into the church alongside men, it appears that some women would disrupt the meetings with inappropriate questions and other unedifying talk. (One sees this phenomenon today, in fact, in churches so enthusiastic about "every-member ministry" and the leveling of all social distinctions that manifestly ungifted people are given the floor to testify or

pray or even preach at length, to the consternation of the congregation.) So Paul tells women, as a general principle that applies to
them as a general class, to ask their husbands at home—implying the
imperative, to be sure, that the husbands have indeed paid attention
to the teaching and can answer those questions! "As in all the churches
of the saints, women should be silent in the churches. For they are not
permitted to speak, but should be subordinate, as the law also says. If
there is anything they desire to know, let them ask their husbands at
home" (1 Cor 14:33-35).[1]

Likewise with leadership: women were not trained to exercise such
public leadership over mixed groups, and society was not trained to
accept it. Women leaders, therefore, would have scandalized their
neighbors. So Paul forbids it in the name of gospel priorities. Indeed,
one of Paul's most direct teachings about the silence and subordination of women, in 1 Timothy 2:11-15, is preceded in that chapter by
this very context of causing as little scandal as possible in order to
bring glory to God and particularly to advantage both evangelism
and the ongoing edification of believers:

> First of all, then, I urge that supplications, prayers, intercessions, and
> thanksgivings be made for everyone, for kings and all who are in high
> positions, so that we may lead a quiet and peaceable life in all god-
> liness and dignity. This is right and is acceptable in the sight of God
> our Savior, who desires everyone to be saved and to come to the
> knowledge of the truth. (1 Tim 2:1-4)

Public *prayer* and *prophecy*, however, do not require formal education. Paul therefore not only allows but actually seems to *expect*
women to engage in such edifying discourse. Thus his only advice to
them on this matter is again to avoid unnecessary scandal—remember,
Paul never minds causing scandal when the heart of the gospel is at
stake!—and therefore to dress as their culture expects them to do, with
their heads covered as a sign of conventional submission to patriarchy.

> But I want you to understand that Christ is the head of every man, and
> the husband is the head of his wife, and God is the head of Christ. Any

man who prays or prophesies with something on his head disgraces his head, but any woman who prays or prophesies with her head unveiled disgraces her head—it is one and the same thing as having her head shaved. For if a woman will not veil herself, then she should cut off her hair; but if it is disgraceful for a woman to have her hair cut off or to be shaved, she should wear a veil. For a man ought not to have his head veiled, since he is the image and reflection of God; but woman is the reflection of man. (1 Cor 11:3-7)

It is intriguing, however, and I think suggestive, that Paul's teaching about gifts and roles in the church is never sorted into gender-specific categories. He never says that all the leaders, all the pastors, all the teachers, and all the evangelists will be men, and that women's gifts reside among the remainder. (I realize that Paul says that an elder is to be "the husband of one wife" [1 Tim 3:2 NASB], but surely his point is faithful monogamy, and not the sex of the elder. Paul is assuming that the elders will be male, for the reasons I am suggesting in this discussion. Pressing this verse to mean that elders *must* be male would, by the same extreme logic, rule out single men as elders, including widowers who had been elders for years.)

Furthermore, if I am correct to suggest that Paul—and God—are not forbidding women from leadership forever and in every circumstance, but are instead temporarily accommodating themselves to the global reality of patriarchy, then we might catch a glimpse of exceptions in the record.[2] Let me make this point as clearly as I can. If there is only one divine teaching—permanent patriarchy—then we would expect this simple rule to be applied everywhere and always by the apostles. But if this teaching were culturally accommodative, and not universal, we might see exceptions even in the early church. We would see anomalies that don't make sense unless they are, indeed, blessed hints of what *could* be and *will* be eventually in the fully present kingdom of God.

We would expect, perhaps, to see *exceptional* women actually teaching adult men—and that is what we do see, in Prisca instructing even someone as gifted as Apollos. We might see *exceptional* women offering leadership through their social standing and wealth—and that is what we do see, in Lydia hosting the local church in her home. We might even see *exceptional* women bearing the titles of eminent leaders in the church, such as "deacon" and "apostle"—and that is what we do see: "I commend to you our sister Phoebe, a deacon of the church at Cenchreae. . . . Greet Andronicus and Junia [a female name], my relatives who were in prison with me; they are prominent among the apostles" (Rom 16:1, 7).[3]

Furthermore, we note the same pattern in later church history. Patriarchy is the rule, but *exceptional* movements and individuals keep emerging. I contend that these exceptions remind us that Christian patriarchy is a divine strategic accommodation to circumstances, and that this accommodation properly gives way when women actually can indeed lead, teach, or otherwise do what a man can do in home and church. Female prophets, learned nuns, powerful abbesses, influential authors, effective missionaries, successful evangelists—and, in our day, eminent pastors and theological scholars: What does this stream of exceptional women tell us?

Well, it might tell us that God is willing to use women if men won't make themselves available for his service. I'm not making this up; some complementarians have argued this way:

> When so many ministers of the stronger and wiser sex are useless or worse than useless in the work of soul saving, and preach for years without being instrumental in a single conversion, is there not a case for woman's ministry? . . . [Yet] had Barak better played the man, Deborah had better played the woman. . . . Had the disciples tarried longer at the sepulchre, Mary need not have been the first proclaimer of our Lord.[4]

This record of women's public ministry, however, could be interpreted another way than as an expedient of divine desperation. The record in fact squares nicely with the model I'm offering here. Where society will not tolerate anything but patriarchy, then the church accommodates itself to that unhappy reality for the greater good of spreading the gospel and, indeed, of simply surviving under the threat of persecution. But where society has open spaces in which Christian women can flourish, they have flourished—and they still do.[5]

To put it more pointedly: when society was patriarchal, as it was in the New Testament context and as it has been everywhere in the world except in modern society in our day, then the church avoided scandal by going along with patriarchy, even as the Bible ameliorated it and made women's situation better than it was under any other culture's gender code. Now, however, that our modern society is at least officially egalitarian, the scandal (ironically enough) is that the church is *not* going along with society, not rejoicing in the unprecedented freedom to let women and men serve according to gift and call without an arbitrary gender line.[6] This scandal of keeping women subordinate to men impedes both the evangelism of others and the edification—the retention and development of faith—of those already converted.[7]

What, then, about the Christian family?

THE FAMILY

Readers who have gotten this far might wonder whether there isn't a kind of sleight-of-hand, or even a sort of theological judo, going on here. I am defending egalitarianism by granting the complementarians almost everything they claim, and then replying that patriarchy is a result of sin in fallen human society, to which God has pragmatically accommodated his people, and not a divinely ordained relationship. Patriarchal gender roles are practiced in the church therefore only as a kind of expedient, an accommodation by the Holy Spirit to deeply embedded practices and attitudes that are to be corrected when the time is ripe. And I then argue that that time has come indeed for most of the readers of this book—not because I somehow discern that this is the "end times," as some enthusiastic egalitarians argue, but for quite a different reason. I am arguing that we need to drop patriarchy as modern Christians because I observe that modern society has become ready to accept homes, churches, and secular institutions that welcome women into all roles, including leadership.

Now how would I come to that sort of conclusion? Why would I possibly think that the Holy Spirit would regard patriarchy as an unjust, even oppressive, structure to which he nonetheless would accommodate himself and the church until such time as both church and society would do away with it? I think so because that's what I think the Holy Spirit has already done in one extremely relevant case: slavery.

The institution of slavery and the institution of patriarchy occur together in at least two key junctures in Christian memory. In nineteenth-century America, abolitionism and feminism were allied for decades—until abolition carried the day (at least officially), and feminism's former allies did not all follow through on the second crusade. Much further back, we encounter slavery and patriarchy linked again, this time in the pages of the New Testament.

Indeed, the social conservatism of the New Testament is exemplified in the linkage of three domestic institutions in several similar passages in the Epistles: slavery, marriage, and parent/child relations. In each case, the apostles condone the relationships of their day, and then ameliorate each one in the light of the gospel. Here is one such passage:

> Wives, be subject to your husbands, as is fitting in the Lord. Husbands, love your wives and never treat them harshly. Children, obey your parents in everything, for this is your acceptable duty in the Lord. Fathers, do not provoke your children, or they may lose heart. Slaves, obey your earthly masters in everything, not only while being watched and in order to please them, but wholeheartedly, fearing the Lord. . . . Masters, treat your slaves justly and fairly, for you know that you also have a Master in heaven. (Col 3:18-22, 4:1[8]; cf. Eph 5:21–6:9; 1 Pet 2:18–3:7—although this last text lacks the parallel of children and parents)

In the case of slavery, modern Christians worldwide have come to agree that the social conservatism of the New Testament was a temporary matter. The early church probably expected Christ to return literally at any moment, so it made no sense for slaves to rise up against masters or for Christians to agitate for slavery's abolition. Christians enjoyed no possibility of success in such a cause, given their tiny numbers. And Christ was coming back to do away with such things momentarily anyhow. Paul therefore encourages slaves to honor their masters precisely in order to forward the cause of the gospel: "Let all who are under the yoke of slavery regard their masters as worthy of all honor, so that the name of God and the teaching may not be blasphemed" (1 Tim 6:1).

As the church accommodated itself over the centuries, however, to the so-called delay of the parousia, or second coming, it gradually began to conclude that the thrust of the Bible regarding the dignity of all people entailed the abolition of slavery. Indeed, some of the very biblical passages that seemed to an earlier age to condone slavery now seemed to all but call for its abolition—the epistle to Philemon being Exhibit A in such an argument. Read with abolitionist eyes, Paul stops just short of commanding Philemon to free Onesimus. And he tells slaves elsewhere, without contradiction of his admonition to slaves to serve well (see also Col 3:24), to gain their freedom if they can (1 Cor 7:21). In the light of these biblical hints directly about slavery, as well as of more general Christian principles, for the first time in history a society voluntarily rid itself of slavery.[9]

Let us not forget that in America this consensus is officially less than 150 years old, and the racism that legitimized slavery has not been eradicated to this day. Indeed, let us remember that preachers on both sides of the slavery controversy marshaled powerful, Bible-based arguments that convinced millions of believers. Some fair-minded observers have concluded that the proslavery forces in fact had the better of this debate, since a straightforward interpretation of these passages regarding slavery conveys no obvious condemnation of that institution and seems instead to encourage Christians in both roles, master and slave, to stay right where they are and simply behave properly.[10] Yet there remains today no important Christian leader anywhere in the modern world who defends slavery. Not one.

Well, what about the other member of the trio, the parent and child relationship? Surely no one would suggest today that this arrangement ought to be revolutionized: that children ought to disobey their parents and that parents are free to abuse their children? Of course not. But no one should suggest, likewise, that children are in perpetual thrall to their parents' commands. The parent/child relationship of this sort is a temporary one that accomplishes certain things in certain circumstances and then is outgrown as the child no longer needs his parents' direction. Indeed, Genesis 2:24 makes it quite clear that part of normal adulthood is leaving father and mother and taking on the parental role oneself in a new household. The obedience of children to parents makes good sense in one situation, and the Bible's authors simply presume that it is obvious that readers should not apply it in every other situation.

I suggest that the same dynamic is true in the husband and wife relationship. In a social situation in which the husband has substantially more power—social, intellectual, political, and financial—because patriarchal society has awarded it to him simply on the basis of his sex, then he should use that power the way all of God's people are supposed to use whatever power they have received: on behalf of others, as imitators of the God who graciously cares for us. Thus the husband is to give generously of his power to benefit his wife, as Christ uses his superior power on behalf of the church, his spouse. This principle helps explain Paul's extended treatment of husband and wife relations in Ephesians 5. Paul begins with a call to mutual submission, since everyone has equal dignity in the Christian fellowship and family. Then (in what seems to some today to be a contradiction) Paul exhorts women to submit to their husbands, and men to care for their wives, in parallel with the relationship of Christ and the church.

> Be subject to one another out of reverence for Christ. Wives, be subject to your husbands as you are to the Lord. For the husband is the head of the wife just as Christ is the head of the church, the body of which he is the Savior. Just as the church is subject to Christ, so also wives ought to be, in everything, to their husbands. Husbands, love your

wives, just as Christ loved the church and gave himself up for her, in order to make her holy by cleansing her with the washing of water by the word, so as to present the church to himself in splendor, without a spot or wrinkle or anything of the kind—yes, so that she may be holy and without blemish. In the same way, husbands should love their wives as they do their own bodies. He who loves his wife loves himself. For no one ever hates his own body, but he nourishes and tenderly cares for it, just as Christ does for the church, because we are members of his body. "For this reason a man will leave his father and mother and be joined to his wife, and the two will become one flesh." This is a great mystery, and I am applying it to Christ and the church. Each of you, however, should love his wife as himself, and a wife should respect her husband. (Eph 5:21-33)

I am arguing that this is exactly the pattern of all of Paul's exhortations: don't try to abolish (now) what can't (now) be abolished, such as patriarchy or slavery, but make the best of it according to all that we know of mutual love in Christ.

In a society such as ours in which patriarchy is no longer everywhere assumed, however, what is the relevance of Ephesians 5 today? Some maintain that it is certainly clear enough at least that wives are to "be subject" to their husbands, but what does that entail?

No complementarian scholar I have encountered seriously advises that husbands make all the decisions in domestic life. Some popular preachers might say so, but they don't realize that such absolute authority and responsibility did not reside in the husband in the ancient world either: wives had a considerable voice in the domestic sphere. Does Paul mean in Ephesians 5 that the husband sets the family policies, perhaps with the advice of his wife, and then she, as a good subordinate, carries them out? Perhaps that's what he means, but it's hard to find complementarian scholars who will argue even this position.

Let me be clear, again, that I recognize the fact on the ground that in many Christian homes the husband and father does wield supreme authority, and that some men do micromanage their wives and families. I recognize that even in more moderate homes, the symbols of authority reside in the male: he leads the conversations, he presides over family worship, he administers discipline, he controls the finances, he has the final say in any important decision, and so on. I recognize also the implicit, but obvious, devaluing of women's competence and authority in such situations. I am not, therefore, claiming that a complementarian position, even a relatively mild one, does not make a difference. Because I believe, on the contrary, that it can make a considerable difference, I am writing this book. What I am arguing just now is that in the *scholarly* literature, one rarely finds defenders of such lopsided patriarchy.

Instead, one finds complementarian teachers telling husbands to make sure that they love their wives self-sacrificially, as Christ loves the church. Such exposition is welcome, to be sure. But we must notice that it avoids the point at issue—it doesn't help us cash out the difference between a loving complementarian marriage and an equally loving egalitarian one. In fact, the only common application of genuine gender distinction in marriage I can find in the complementarian literature today is the "breaking the deadlock" hypothetical: if the mutually respectful husband and wife cannot come to a decision together that needs to be made, then the husband is to cast the deciding vote.

Such a reading of this passage strikes me, frankly, as ludicrous. If Paul, a master of the Greek language, had intended to communicate this idea, then surely he could have been more plain about it! Indeed, is Paul really saying something like this? "Be mutually submissive, but whenever you can't finally agree on something important, then make sure that the husband decides—just as when Christ and the church discuss things, and they can't agree, the nod goes to Christ." Seriously?

Furthermore, when I have asked complementarian couples how often in years or even decades of marriage they have ever had to resort to this device, the answer almost invariably comes back, never. So, I respond, are we really supposed to think that the Holy Spirit inspired the apostle Paul to write this relatively extended section of this holy epistle to command, however obscurely, a principle that is almost never actually applicable?

I conclude that it is better to see this passage in parallel with slave-holding and parenting. Society has already awarded power to masters, parents, and husbands. Those are given, and massive, social facts. Paul does not advise a domestic revolution that would upset all of these relationships, but instead commands Christians to ameliorate these exercises of power as far as they can. And, along the way, the Holy Spirit inspires him to plant seeds of emancipation that blossom when the time is right.[11]

Another notorious passage regarding gender can be understood this same way. The apostle Peter describes women as the "weaker sex"—or, in the King James Version's memorable rendering, the "weaker vessel" (1 Pet 3:7). But it is not clear that Peter is asserting something universal about women, something essential about them, as if all women everywhere and always are "weaker" than all men. Indeed, that seems to be obvious nonsense, so let us look for an alternative interpretation! What is not nonsensical, sadly, is that in a patriarchal society, Peter is telling the simple truth: economically, politically, legally, educationally—when it comes to most dimensions of social power, women *are* weaker than men.[12] So he advises the Christian wife to play her role well and to expect her husband to play his, to their mutual benefit.

Let us be sure to note also that Peter exhorts the wife to be submissive precisely because of gospel priorities and, I think we can fairly assume, because he recognizes that marriage conventions of his time are not ready to be altered in any radically egalitarian way. What he does *not* say is that wives should submit to their husbands because he believes in some sort of essential submissiveness supposedly endemic to being a woman. Instead, the good of the gospel is primarily in view: "Wives, in the same way, accept the authority of your husbands, so that, even if some of them do not obey the word, they may be won over without a word by their wives' conduct, when they see the purity and reverence of your lives" (1 Pet 3:1-2; cf. Tit 2:4-5).

Likewise, Peter exhorts the stronger (men) to use their socially inherited privileges in order to care for the weaker (women). Indeed, Peter says that husbands are to behave "in the same way"—an extraordinarily surprising phrase. He is saying, "according to the same principles of new life in Christ, according to the same gospel priorities, according to the same Lord who tells your wife to submit to you," you had better—what? You had better "be considerate as you live with your wives, and treat them with respect as the weaker partner and as heirs with you of the gracious gift of life" (1 Pet 3:7 NIV). So far from granting a license to abuse or exploit, or even just to boss around as chattel, Peter lays on husbands the command to consider and respect their wives, their fellow Christians, and on pain of the husbands' very relationship with God: "so that nothing will hinder your prayers." In this principle, of course, Peter echoes Paul's teaching about pastoral leaders acting as servants ("slaves") of their churches, and implies Christ's own striking example of those with power being willing to stoop so low as to wash another's feet—or even to die on a cross for him or her.[13]

So long as you are the stronger member of any relationship, the apostles say, use that strength on behalf of the weaker; so long as you are the weaker, God tells you that it is best to submit to the stronger. The fact that you occupy a particular social role currently, however, implies nothing about whether that role is legitimate or about whether you will remain in it indefinitely. Again, it is suggestive that the obviously temporary roles of parents and children are linked several times in Scripture with roles that the ancients would have seen as timeless features of the social landscape: masters and slaves, husbands and wives, men and women.

The Pattern of Doubleness

SINCE WE'RE TAKING ON THE MOST DIFFICULT texts for egalitarians, let us consider a suggestive pattern that appears in one of the most difficult texts in the Old Testament, and then recurs in a number of the most difficult texts in the New.

> The LORD spoke to Moses, saying: Speak to the people of Israel, saying: If a woman conceives and bears a male child, she shall be ceremonially unclean seven days; as at the time of her menstruation, she shall be unclean. On the eighth day the flesh of his foreskin shall be circumcised. Her time of blood purification shall be thirty-three days; she shall not touch any holy thing, or come into the sanctuary, until the days of her purification are completed. If she bears a female child, she shall be unclean two weeks, as in her menstruation; her time of blood purification shall be sixty-six days. (Lev 12:1-5)

There are at least two major matters here in light of our concerns. First, it appears that menstruation and bearing children—two of the experiences of womanhood that are glorified in much feminist literature—are disparaged in the Bible. Indeed, they are forms of impurity that require temporary quarantine. Uh-oh: here's the bad old Bible once again demeaning female bodies.

Yet a few chapters later, in Leviticus 15, it appears that the matter is not the uncleanness of a woman's body per se, but of any human body that discharges fluids. The man who has an otherwise-undescribed discharge is likewise unclean, as is the man who has a seminal discharge. So in fact there is no sexism here. The matter at stake is the common ancient Near Eastern concern for ritual purity and bodily integrity, not a disparagement of women.

The second matter is the disparate time required for purification in the case of a male child versus a female child. Indeed, the latter is twice that of the former, in both the case of personal uncleanness and of so-called blood purification. Doesn't this indicate that the Torah holds men to be twice as important as women?

There is no doubt that the Torah is a patriarchal text. Men have the legal, political, and economic power over women, children, slaves, animals, lands—everything. And that power is never called into question. But two observations must also be made. First, the Torah is not, in Christian eyes, God's ultimate word on human society. Old Testament scholar Iain Provan illuminates this point:

> The law must always be read in the context of the creation purposes of God, because Old Testament law seems to be aimed at dealing often with ugly reality as it is, rather than enunciating ideal principles of conduct. That is what modern law does, too. It does not prescribe virtue; it deals with ugly reality as it actually is. . . . [The laws regarding men and women are] attempts to regulate what otherwise would be even worse situations for the woman concerned.[1]

Indeed, Jesus reminds his Jewish audience of that in his preaching, as he cautions that much of Torah was accommodated to the sinfulness of Israel and that he is now calling Israel to a much higher standard of righteousness:

> Some Pharisees came to him, and to test him they asked, "Is it lawful for a man to divorce his wife for any cause?" He answered, "Have you not read that the one who made them at the beginning 'made them male and female,' and said, 'For this reason a man shall leave his father and mother and be joined to his wife, and the two shall become one flesh'? So they are no longer two, but one flesh. Therefore what God has joined together, let no one separate." They said to him, "Why then did Moses command us to give a certificate of dismissal and to divorce her?" He said to them, "It was because you were so hard-hearted that

Moses allowed you to divorce your wives, but from the beginning it was not so. And I say to you, whoever divorces his wife, except for unchastity, and marries another commits adultery." (Mt 19:3-9)

So the Torah is not to be understood by the church as a blueprint for Christian conduct. It is to be read as Scripture, yes—as "inspired by God and . . . useful for teaching, for reproof, for correction, and for training in righteousness" (2 Tim 3:16). But just *how* it is to be useful for us is a question of careful hermeneutics. And my sense is that these sorts of passages in Torah are illustrative of God's accommodation to something he does not like, namely, patriarchy, and thus also his simultaneous amelioration of it. For scholars indicate that the treatment of women in the Law is no worse, and frequently better, than the ancient Near Eastern parallels.[2]

The second observation to be made about Torah leads us to the intriguing pattern of doubleness that I see in similar New Testament texts as well: the customary privileging of the male in the very same context as the perhaps surprising affirmation of male and female as equal.

Let's return to this Leviticus passage about childbirth. Yes, bearing a female child renders the mother ceremonially impure for twice as long as if she had born a male child. But the passage quoted above goes right on as follows:

When the days of her purification are completed, *whether for a son or for a daughter*, she shall bring to the priest at the entrance of the tent of meeting a lamb in its first year for a burnt offering, and a pigeon or a turtledove for a sin offering. He shall offer it before the LORD, and make atonement on her behalf; then she shall be clean from her flow of blood. This is the law for her who bears a child, *male or female.* (Lev 12:6-7)

Another highly problematic example is found in Exodus 21, but it has a similar pattern. It is too long to quote here, but it is a complex interweaving of *both* the standard privileging of men *and* of the affirmation of men and women as equal to each other (including male and female slaves and children).

We can find this similar pattern of doubleness in some of the key New Testament texts regarding gender. Let's examine them in turn.

As Paul comes to the end of his discussion of head coverings in 1 Corinthians 11, he concludes in patriarchal style:

> For a man ought not to have his head veiled, since he is the image and reflection of God; but woman is the reflection of man. Indeed, man was not made from woman, but woman from man. Neither was man created for the sake of woman, but woman for the sake of man. For this reason a woman ought to have a symbol of authority on her head, because of the angels. (1 Cor 11:7-10)

I shan't tackle verse 10 regarding "the angels," since two thousand years of commentary on this verse have not proved especially illuminating. But the rest of the passage seems pretty typical of a first-century rabbi who is reading Genesis 1 and 2 through patriarchal lenses—lenses that not all of us share, of course. Indeed, as many Bible scholars have pointed out, Paul's interpretation of woman as the reflection of the man, and not directly of God as his image, seems to fly in the face of Genesis 1:26-27. And his depiction of the second creation story, that of Genesis 2, of the woman as being created from and for the man, seems more than a bit tendentious. The *adam* was not obviously sexed before the division into male and female, the rejoining of which division is clearly in view in the "two become one flesh" vision of marriage at the end of that chapter. The woman is created as a partner, an *ezer*. This word is usually translated "helper," and is used generally in the Old Testament of God himself as "helper" of his people. Thus the fundamental concept seems to be that the woman is a partner and companion for the man, not a subordinate to the man.

Similar problems emerge in exegeting the oft-cited 1 Timothy 2 passage: "For Adam was formed first, then Eve; and Adam was not deceived, but the woman was deceived and became a transgressor" (1 Tim 2:13-14). Again Paul ignores Genesis 1, in which male and female are created at the same time as the image of God together.

Then we see that his argument from Genesis 2 that the prior creation of the man entails some sort of *political* superiority seems not obviously to be taught in that chapter itself.[3]

As for verse 14, Paul might seem to be suggesting that all women are more prone to spiritual deception than all men, and thus they should be silent in church. But this interpretation seems preposterous coming from a man with such obvious regard for Priscilla and numerous other wise women in the church he gladly affirms by name (see the greetings in Rom 16). And then verse 15 seems to suggest that salvation will come through childbirth, which makes any serious reader wonder whether Paul has been working metaphorically all along, since of course he cannot be read as actually meaning that women receive eternal life merely by faithfully giving birth.

Just what to make of Paul's deployment of these brief, allusive, and ad hoc arguments, then—rather than what he says in his extended reflections—is a vexed area of hermeneutical scholarship. And that is simply a scholar's way of saying, This is a very strange passage on which there is very little agreement.[4] On it, therefore, I can shed no definitive light. So I will concede that it is easy to read some of these verses as supporting patriarchy everywhere and always, as complementarians have done. But I will maintain that one does not have to read them that way, especially since to do so means to understand Paul to be making a number of strange interpretative moves, including applying Genesis in ways that seem not at all obvious in those texts themselves. I remind my complementarian friends, moreover, that the task before us is to make sense of *all* that Paul says, not just a few bits we happen to think are clear in the midst of otherwise murky passages, including the apparently egalitarian verses—some of which appear *in the same place.*

Can we somehow avoid becoming mired in these questions? Let us first concede that Paul is indeed maintaining a patriarchal line, whatever one makes of his arguments for it. Then let's go on to notice what Paul says immediately following his argument in 1 Corinthians 11: "Nevertheless, in the Lord woman is not independent of man or man independent of woman. For just as woman came from man, so man comes through woman; but all things come from God" (1 Cor 11:11-12). Paul seems to have brought himself up short with the "nevertheless." I wonder whether he felt he was on the verge of pressing patriarchy too far. So he then does what he does elsewhere: emphasize mutuality and equal dignity between the sexes. Paul therefore follows the same double pattern that we saw in the Torah: affirm some sort of patriarchal conduct, but then also affirm the fundamental equality of men and women in a way that can be seen, in different circumstances, to provide the grounds for egalitarianism.

Consider also the long passage in Ephesians 5 about husbands and wives, in which this pattern is inverted. I need to say at the outset that I have trouble buying the common egalitarian argument about this passage—namely, that Paul is really saying the same thing in two different ways. Egalitarians often suggest that he is teaching husbands and wives to treat each other equally and identically, but using very different language in each case—as if perhaps he is pulling wives up from their degradation with one hand and pulling down husbands from their position of false power with the other. If this is what Paul is saying, however, we now repeat the charge we made earlier in the opposite direction: this master of Greek seems to have an oddly roundabout way of putting this simple point. And the Holy Spirit has somehow failed to help the church see that point through two thousand years of Christian domestic patriarchy.

Instead, the parallel Paul draws with Christ and the church—who are not equal, in both fact and role—seems strongly to militate against any simple sense of equivalence here. Furthermore, the typical egalitarian argument that Jesus models submission and self-abnegation in his service to the church is true, of course, but not "true enough." Such a Christology presents a truncated picture: Jesus is also Lord of the church, the one who gives commands to the church and who expects worship from the church—even as he provides self-sacrificially for the church.

Thus I think Paul is playing off the wonderful paradox of the One who is both Lord and Servant of the church in order to provide a splendid model for husbands to love their wives, from whatever may be their analogical positions of social power, with Christlike affection and self-sacrifice.

Having maintained, then, the patriarchal side of the "doubleness" we keep noticing (albeit it is invariably an importantly mitigated patriarchy), let us observe the egalitarian side as well, as seen in how the whole long passage begins: "Be subject to one another out of reverence for Christ" (Eph 5:21). Indeed, the following passage distinguishing wives and husbands grammatically depends on this verse that unites them: the very verb, "be subject," is missing in verse 22, as verse 22 assumes verse 21. Thus the exhortation to wives to "submit" is linked at the very level of syntax to *mutual* submission.

This double pattern appears again in 1 Peter, and it perhaps is worth reviewing this whole passage to see the irrefutable call to conform to patriarchy combined with an incipient egalitarianism.

> Wives, in the same way, accept the authority of your husbands, so that, even if some of them do not obey the word, they may be won over without a word by their wives' conduct, when they see the purity and reverence of your lives. Do not adorn yourselves outwardly by braiding your hair, and by wearing gold ornaments or fine clothing; rather, let your adornment be the inner self with the lasting beauty of a gentle and quiet spirit, which is very precious in God's sight. It was in this way long ago that the holy women who hoped in God used to adorn themselves by accepting the authority of their husbands. Thus Sarah obeyed Abraham and called him lord. You have become her daughters as long as you do what is good and never let fears alarm you. Husbands, in the same way, show consideration for your wives in your life together, paying honor to the woman as the weaker sex, *since they too are also heirs of the gracious gift of life*—so that nothing may hinder your prayers. (1 Pet 3:1-7)[5]

It is this "doubleness," therefore, that is the key to the gender model I am offering here. And it is the main difference between my model and the "redemptive trajectory" or "redemptive movement" hermeneutic more typical of biblical feminists. They see a single, upward line in the Bible, a line of progressive amelioration of oppression. This trend, they believe, ought to be extended beyond the end of the apostolic era to our own day so that it will result in full emancipation—of slaves, women, and other victims of sinful hierarchy.

To be sure, I see the amelioration that they see in the Bible. The regard for women, children, foreigners, and slaves in the Old Testament law is far better than it is in any other ancient Near Eastern civilization that we know of. But I do not see a single, upward line that would make Jesus and Paul virtual egalitarians. Instead, I see a *double* message almost from the beginning of the Bible and showing up right through the New Testament. In regard to slavery, for example, Paul both counsels acquiescence and even enthusiastic service on the part of slaves (Col 3:22-24) and also barely stops short of ordering Philemon outright to free Onesimus. An even more conspicuous pattern of doubleness is evident in regard to gender, as we have seen, from the Torah through Jesus to Peter and Paul. The New Testament is not a uniformly egalitarian text, and not even a just-on-the-verge-of-egalitarian text, but one that contains numerous instances of these two messages, often side by side.

Why does noticing this pattern matter? Without acknowledging this doubleness, one cannot make sense of the longstanding Christian defenses of slaveholding and patriarchy—unless one believes that all of our fellow Christians who have held slaves or have espoused patriarchy have been guilty of patently bad Bible reading in the interest of some evil agenda. I think it makes more sense of the Scriptures and of church history to acknowledge that there *were* biblical arguments available to Christians of both of those views.

So why prefer the egalitarian reading to the patriarchal one? Because the egalitarian interpretation makes better sense of the presence of *both kinds* of texts alongside each other in Scripture. The egalitarian reading does not disrespect the traditional reading as if it had no basis in the Bible. It clearly does. But egalitarians see God working through patriarchal structures in Scripture and in church history while also providing the foundation for the removal of those structures when and where the cause of the gospel would be advanced thereby.

In our society, there is no downside to the full functional equality of women, no scandal that would ensue that would harm the church's central mission of proclaiming the gospel. The two messages—of patriarchy and of equality—are both there in the Bible. But the former, I suggest, is an accommodation in order to advance God's mission via Israel and then via the church. Once that accommodation is no longer needed, the first message can, and must, give way to the second.

What Then?

I RECOGNIZE THAT MY COMPLEMENTARIAN friends might have become exasperated during this argument. "We don't deny women's equality!" they will say. "We affirm that the sexes are entirely equal in God's regard and in ours. We just think that they are to play different roles. These passages you cite make exactly *our* point, not yours!"

But then we have to consider this question: Why would God call entirely equal sexes to deeply different roles, ever and always, world without end? Why indeed would one role be that of leadership and the other of submission, if women and men are not only equal in status and dignity before God but equal in every other way as well?

Not so long ago in the West, and not so far away in the world even today, patriarchy made sense because it was assumed that women were indeed inferior in ways pertinent to leadership. Such was the world of the New Testament church, as it has been in most times and places. Women were understood to be less rational, more emotional, less courageous, more sentimental, less objective, more intuitive, and so on. Thus it made sense for men to dominate and women to submit— just as it made the same sort of sense for white people to dominate everyone else they encountered in the age of spreading empire if everyone else was understood to be inferior and even subhuman.[1]

Many complementarians do not want to argue that way today, however. Most people recognize the social-scientific data demonstrating that many women do, in fact, surpass many men in every important respect, from intelligence (however understood) to morality (however understood) to psychological health (however understood) to physical prowess (however understood).[2] Many more women are evidently the peers of their male colleagues—in society, yes, and in church and home. Women do remain generally physically smaller than men, but why in a modern society would a broad tendency to "be bigger" have anything to do with restricting leadership to men in home, church, or anyplace else, even as a general principle? To pursue this logic to absurdity, what about the individual women who are taller and stronger than all the men nearby? Shouldn't they then lead that particular group? In fact, should we institute armwrestling to see who will become the next chief of surgery, or law partner, or bishop?

Whatever gender differences remain between men and women, they seem to have nothing to do with one sex exercising leadership over the other in society, church, or home. I suggest, therefore, that the complementarian position has become incoherent.[3] Thanks be to God that many complementarians are *not* sexists who believe that women are inferior to men. (Now, to those who maintain that women really are inferior in these important respects, I won't pause to say much, except that the Bible, reason, and experience are against you. All you have on your side are a few misogynist texts scattered here and there in the Christian theological tradition and tendentious readings of the very texts of Scripture I have shown to be *not* describing women as intrinsically inferior.) To these mainstream complementarians who do believe that women are equal and yet who see the Bible as restricting leadership to men, let me respectfully and fraternally ask, *Why would God mandate that pattern—forever?* May I invite you to consider the Bible in the way I am suggesting instead, which does, I think, make better sense of the elements of both patriarchy and equality that occur in these many relevant passages, as well as making better sense of the common sense we have regarding the capabilities of women alongside men today.

Indeed, as Howard Marshall pointedly suggests, the very term *complementarian* may be nonsense: two classes of people are equally capable, but certain leadership roles are reserved to just one of those classes, yet everything else can be done by members of either class—what is "complementary" about that arrangement? (Only the bearing and suckling of babies is reserved for women, which is hardly what anyone means by "complementary.")[4]

Terminological wobbles aside, the fundamental practical question today is this: What is God calling Christians to do in regard to gender when society itself shifts to egalitarianism? I am arguing that there no longer remains any rationale for the woman to remain in the once-expected role of dependence and submission—just as there isn't any rationale for the grown-up child to keep acting as if he requires his parents' direction as he did when he was little. When, under the providence of God and the ongoing, spreading influence of kingdom values, society opens up to the abolition of slavery or the emancipation of women, then Christians can rejoice and, indeed, be in the vanguard of such change—as we *have* been in both causes. The dark irony remains today, I repeat, precisely in Christians lagging behind society and still requiring a submissive role for women—a posture that now is a scandalous mirror image of the scandal that egalitarianism would have caused in the patriarchal first century.

This, then, is the model of gender I submit for your consideration. It makes the most sense to me of what for many have appeared to be contradictions in Scripture, in church history, and in life today in the modern world. In the next chapter, let's test this model by exposing it to the best counterarguments we can find.

Counterarguments from Theology

BECAUSE THE PARADIGM I HAVE OFFERED HERE is neither complementarian nor typically egalitarian, it can be challenged from both sides. Let's consider, then, a variety of arguments to see how well this paradigm stands up to such questioning.

As we do so, we will remember one of the principles of sound theological method that we established early on: the task of Christian theology is not to arrive at the one, timeless, seamless answer that fits everything nicely into place without strain and without remainder. The task instead is to formulate an interpretation that does the best job, relative to the other options available, of explaining most of the most important data, and as much of the remainder as possible. The fact, then, that my paradigm does not explain a particular detail as well as does another interpretation must be acknowledged in the interests of both Christian honesty and the humble openness we should all maintain in hopes of having our ideas improved. For if I dismiss a contrary datum or interpretation, explain it away, or otherwise circumvent it, I miss an opportunity to reconsider and reconstruct my interpretation for the better. But the fact that my paradigm does not explain every detail as well as does another interpretation in any particular case doesn't mean that it isn't overall the best one that is currently available. And if it is the best one available, then it is the one we ought to adopt.[1]

I have tried to deal fairly with arguments from particular Scriptures in the foregoing discussions. Now we can encounter other sorts of arguments: from theology, from church history, and from contemporary experience and practice. We begin with theology.

The relations among members of the Trinity demonstrate how men and women should treat each other.

The first, and perhaps last, troubling thing to notice here is that this argument is deployed by both complementarians and egalitarians. Both sides, that is, think that they can win points by referring questions of (human) gender to the doctrine of the Trinity. So if both sides think that x proves their point, then likely x isn't going to be terribly helpful.

Such references to the Trinity in gender debates by orthodox Christians, of course, generally are not in regard to the gender of God or of the various members of the Godhead. The issue is the political question, so to speak, of initiative and response, authority and subordination, leadership and submission. What does the doctrine of the Trinity, and particularly its construal of the relations among the members of the Godhead, teach us about how men and women are to relate to each other?

All orthodox Christians affirm that the members of the Trinity are indeed coequal. We also affirm that the Son and Spirit willingly submit to the Father. Moreover, we affirm that the Spirit humbly bears witness, not to himself, but to the Son. The Athanasian Creed, widely recited in the global church, goes to great lengths to make these points:

5. For there is one person of the Father, another of the Son, and another of the Holy Spirit.

6. But the Godhead of the Father, of the Son, and of the Holy Spirit is all one, the glory equal, the majesty coeternal.

7. Such as the Father is, such is the Son, and such is the Holy Spirit.

8. The Father uncreated, the Son uncreated, and the Holy Spirit uncreated.

9. The Father incomprehensible, the Son incomprehensible, and the Holy Spirit incomprehensible.

10. The Father eternal, the Son eternal, and the Holy Spirit eternal.

11. And yet they are not three eternals but one eternal.

12. As also there are not three uncreated nor three incomprehensible, but one uncreated and one incomprehensible.

13. So likewise the Father is almighty, the Son almighty, and the Holy Spirit almighty.

14. And yet they are not three almighties, but one almighty.

15. So the Father is God, the Son is God, and the Holy Spirit is God;

16. And yet they are not three Gods, but one God.

17. So likewise the Father is Lord, the Son Lord, and the Holy Spirit Lord;

18. And yet they are not three Lords but one Lord.

19. For like as we are compelled by the Christian verity to acknowledge every Person by himself to be God and Lord;

20. So are we forbidden by the catholic religion to say, There are three Gods or three Lords.

21. The Father is made of none, neither created nor begotten.

22. The Son is of the Father alone; not made nor created, but begotten.

23. The Holy Spirit is of the Father and of the Son; neither made, nor created, nor begotten, but proceeding.

24. So there is one Father, not three Fathers; one Son, not three Sons; one Holy Spirit, not three Holy Spirits.

25. And in this Trinity none is afore or after another; none is greater or less than another.

26. But the whole three persons are coeternal, and coequal.

27. So that in all things, as aforesaid, the Unity in Trinity and the Trinity in Unity is to be worshipped.

28. He therefore that will be saved must thus think of the Trinity.[2]

Complementarians have argued, then, that the Trinity shows us that women can submit to men without feeling automatically devalued. In the Trinity, subordination does not imply inferiority, so no one should bridle at the proposal that women should be subordinate to men.

Egalitarians prefer to argue from the coequality of members of the Trinity to the opposite conclusion that the members of the Trinity in fact play different roles, but none of them dominates the others. Indeed, they are all involved in all aspects of divine work, from creation through redemption to consummation, in an interplay of mutual joy and cooperation. As no member of the coequal Trinity rules the others, so neither human sex should rule the other.

For my part, I think the complementarians get the better of this sort of argument. The Father is always pictured in the Bible in the supreme position vis-à-vis the other members of the Trinity. It is to the Father that Jesus prays, and it is to the Father that he instructs us to pray in the Lord's Prayer. It is the Father to whom the Son always defers. And the Holy Spirit is sent by the Father in the name of the Son.[3]

The problem I have with the complementarian reference to the Trinity in regard to gender is that it is a bad theological move to attempt—by *anyone*, on *any* side of this issue. Any strong parallels between the inner life of the Trinity and human relationships just aren't there. For one obvious thing, the Trinity is/are three and when it comes to gender we are instead talking about two. For another, the divine Father and Son are depicted as, yes, two males, and even the biblical pronouns for the Spirit are masculine—even though our theology reminds us that neither God nor any of the members of the Godhead is actually male.[4] Finally, it is in Genesis 1 that we encounter the introduction of the idea of human beings—male and female—created in the image of God. And in this passage there is no explicit reference to the Trinity at all. Indeed, nowhere in the Bible does an author draw permanent implications from the nature of the Trinity to human relations.

To be sure, Paul does link Christ's subordination to the Father to the woman's subordination to the man in that odd passage in 1 Corinthians regarding head coverings—on which practice, interestingly, virtually no defender of patriarchy in North America today wants to insist even as they fasten on this passage to assert patriarchy itself: "But I want you to realize that the head of every man is Christ, and the head of the woman is man, and the head of Christ is God" (1 Cor 11:3 NIV). In the context Paul is addressing, patriarchy is indeed affirmed by the pattern of Christ's deference to the Father. And one key implication of the passage is that women do not have to feel that they are less valued by God because they are called to submit to their husbands, for Christ our example has submitted fully to his Father. Whether, however, Paul (and the Holy Spirit) intends to go beyond this justification of Christians submitting for the gospel's sake to the current social custom of patriarchy to decree patriarchy as an *eternal* principle of gender relations is exactly what my model disputes.

Many theologians (I among them) strongly endorse circumspection when it comes to the general principle of trying to use one of the great mysteries of the faith—the internal life of God in the Trinity—to shed light on some other doctrine. Some doctrines certainly do require deployment of the doctrine of the Trinity, especially Christology, soteriology, and pneumatology. We cannot articulate those central doctrines, and the narratives that gave rise to them, without the doctrine of the Trinity. Indeed, it was the attempt by the early Christians to make sense of their experiences of Jesus and the Holy Spirit that drove them to trinitarian formulations in the first place.[5] But the question of gender seems to be one of those theological subjects not much improved by reference to the Trinity—as is evidenced by the fact that everyone seems to be able to selectively access this doctrine in the interest of contradictory understandings of gender. In short, I find this whole line of theological reasoning unhelpful, and therefore neither an obstacle nor a boon to my investigation of gender.

Worse, however, is my sense that invoking the Trinity here, as both sides do, could be seen as rather manipulatively attempting to add a giant trump card—the Trinity itself!—to make commonsensical points, and that bringing the Trinity into the discussion to make those points doesn't mean one's overarching interpretation of gender is correct. We don't need to peer into the mystery of the inner life of God to know that equals can play different roles, including hierarchical ones. Just look at any football team and notice how the same player always tells the other players what to do without any of those other players complaining about his rights being violated or his dignity besmirched. Look at any hospital operating room, or into any cabinet meeting, and a clear hierarchy of people who esteem each other nonetheless as fully human, talented, worthy of respect, and so on is just obvious and unproblematic. So it seems to me to be frankly a little fishy to drag the doctrine of the Trinity into this conversation.

The submission of wives to husbands and the care of husbands for wives provides an important picture of the relationship of God with Israel and, later, of Christ with the church. To assert an equal partnership of women with men today thus recklessly disposes of this lovely and important pattern of how God relates to God's people.

There can be no disputing this basic observation of the way God has depicted his relationship with his people in the Bible. God wonderfully took up the best traits of masculinity in ancient cultures to tell believers important things about his love, and power, and initiative, and faithfulness on their behalf. He also modeled for them, thereby, how husbands were to treat their wives in such cultures—as Paul argues at some length in Ephesians 5 regarding Christ and the church.[6]

There are notable passages in the Bible that speak of God's "femaleness" (specifically as a mother bird, e.g., Deut 32:11; Mt 23:37). But let us recall that the latter of those references is uttered by a male human being, Jesus. Thus we cannot press such metaphors very far at all regarding gender and God. There is simply no doubt that the dominant biblical portrait of God is drawn with masculine imagery. So what is a culturally and personally sensitive theologian to do with what seems, frankly, to be an embarrassment? Why did God reveal Godself almost all the time as "himself" and not "herself" or "itself" or "him/herself"?

Even those of us who maintain a traditional understanding of inspiration believe that in the Bible God accommodates his ideas and ways to our little human minds and hearts. That is, the Bible doesn't tell us about the Most High God in God's own self, for that would be beyond our understanding. The Bible, as God's Word *to us*, speaks of God as God is to, and toward, us. Now, if we try to "think God's thoughts after him,"[7] why might God select this sort of language almost all the time for self-description?

I suggest that from the beginning of revelation God has tried to get two main points about Godself across to human beings. The first is that God is transcendent, almighty, self-existent; the creator and sustainer of all things, author of history, upholder of righteousness, judge of the earth, consummator of the ages. Now, how would God best communicate this point to people in the cultures of the Old and New Testaments—and, indeed, to most people in history around the world? By using the image of "lord," of ruler, monarch, judge, master—all of which were positions generally held by males.

The second and complementary point God has tried to get across to us is that God cares deeply about human beings as well as the rest of creation. God made us, looks after us, disciplines us, and draws us into renewed fellowship with Godself. In particular, God chooses and cherishes a people, establishes with them a covenant of care, and seeks to forge with them an eternal bond of faithful, mutual devotion. How would God best get this point across to people in the cultures of the Old and New Testaments—and, indeed, to most people in history around the world? By using the image of "lover"—of father, yes, and also in terms of suitor and husband. In cultures in which men take the initiative in courtship, having to woo and win the bride (normally with the consent of her parents, of course), the image of a male suitor works most naturally. In cultures in which husbands and fathers rule their households and provide materially for them and defend them, the masculine image of "lord" works most naturally.

If Yahweh instead had a consort like Asherah, he would have a divine counterpart to love. Thus the striking, even scandalous, biblical image of God seeking a bride in the people of Israel would make no sense. And if God were to reveal Godself as asexual or as simultaneously and "equally" masculine and feminine, there again would be no grounds on which to relate God to humanity in the tender and ardent image of a spouse.

Does this imagery of suitor and husband mean that God in some fundamental sense *needs* his people the way human husbands need their wives? Do God's joy and fulfillment really depend on the faithful devotion of his spouse? Many Christians harrumph at this point and say, No! God needs nothing, and he certainly doesn't need us.

Well, the Bible seems to say that he *does* need us, in some important way. In fact, the Bible seems to say it often: "As the bridegroom rejoices over the bride, so shall your God rejoice over you" (Is 62:5). "Husbands, love your wives, just as Christ loved the church and gave himself up for her. . . . For no one ever hates his own body, but he nourishes and tenderly cares for it, just as Christ does for the church" (Eph 5:25, 29). Metaphysical affirmations (such as God's "aseity") notwithstanding, God has bound himself to his people with love, and it is the love of (one speaks carefully here) companions, and supremely of husbands and wives.

God clearly is the greater partner in the relationship. It would be inappropriate, however, exclusively to use the language of parent and child. Though this terminology does depict some aspects of the divine/human relationship, it does not convey God's complete investment in, and hope for, a lifelong relationship of mutuality. Nor does such imagery call us to grow up and realize our full potential. Surely only marriage imagery can work this way, and in cultures that included both mutuality and hierarchy in male/female relations (which is again to say, most cultures), only "lord" and "lover" imagery would work. So the question is this: If you had been God then, what would you have done to convey these ideas?[8]

Perhaps this brief reflection raises a cautionary note regarding the semantics of our theology, liturgy, and so on. Changing an element here often means an implicit change there, and one that we might not, in fact, want to make. Yes, we need to affirm—and perhaps affirm more often than we do—that God is not male. We need to recognize that the biblical accounts need reinterpretation from points of view other than that of the traditional privileged male. But let us also appreciate the multidimensional images of the Bible that contain important truths in helpful, balanced combination—such as the language of "lord" and "lover." If we egalitarians are going to go beyond culture-bound biblical images as we attempt to theologize in contemporary, nonpatriarchal terms, we must make sure that our alternatives maintain the best elements of the biblical system and do so in their appropriate relations. This is always the challenge in any attempt to improve on the tradition of our elders (let alone on the revelation of God!): it often emerges that they knew more than we might think, and we would do well not to dispense inadvertently, let alone peremptorily, with their wisdom.

Yet the semantic problem remains for those of us in modern society, in which the symbols have changed their meanings. When patriarchy is now odious and retains few of the positive connotations of its ancient heritage on which the biblical portraits depend, and when women and men are treated as equals so that we no longer reflect anything of the vast difference between God and his people that previously was reflected by patriarchal marriage—does it make sense to carry on this symbolism? I doubt that God wants us to continue in what is now a deeply problematic drama, a drama that to many people today—both within the church and without—bespeaks a Deity's domination of his inferiors, rather than the intended message of our gracious Lord's care for his dependents.

So let us be clear: by maintaining egalitarianism in our place and time, we must not simply discard these inspiring pictures of God's care for his people as if they are merely outdated and therefore irrelevant to our situation. We gladly read them in the Bible, embedded as they are in patriarchal cultures in which they made good sense. We should gratefully retrieve them from the Bible, and translate them for our edification in a different, egalitarian culture with hermeneutical sensitivity so that we may hear what God is and isn't saying here and now, as well as there and then, in such a depiction of himself and his beloved.

The pastor is a priest, an intermediary between God and his people. Thus he stands in for Christ, the great Mediator, and only a male person can properly represent Christ in this role since Christ was male.

Roman Catholics have argued this way for a long time, given their particular sacramental understanding of priesthood. As a Protestant, however, I do not share this vision of what it means to serve as *pastor* of a church. I also defend the Protestant affirmation of the *priesthood* of *all* believers—not just clergy and not just males. Any of us Christians can, and should, be ready to hear the confession of a fellow believer and pronounce words of gospel healing to him or her—which is what Luther meant, after all, by "the priesthood of all believers." So this argument doesn't count for me. Furthermore, I find it extremely odd that any other Protestant would take it seriously—as some apparently do.[9]

Were I persuaded, however, of this view of pastor-as-priest in the role of intermediary, I *still* would not find this argument compelling. For why is it Jesus Christ's maleness that must be figured in the person of the priest? Why not his Jewishness—and so much for Gentiles? Or his singleness (I realize that this is exactly the Roman Catholic argument for clerical celibacy!)? Does a priest have to be of early middle age (no younger or older priests, please) or be entirely able-bodied (no room here for disabled clergy), and so on? The strongest argument that can be made for the significance of the maleness of Jesus and then of priests is, indeed, much like the previous argument: that maleness in a patriarchal culture bespeaks something important about God and God's representatives. But what about in an egalitarian society? If the symbol no longer works, because maleness no longer automatically correlates culturally with this or that personal trait or social position, it seems not just pointless, but needlessly scandalous, to retain it.

I acknowledge that because I do not understand the pastoral ministry in this sense of functioning as an intermediary, I may well be missing something important here. Still, as I have said, this argument strikes me as pointless even within the circles that do see pastors in this priestly role. And it certainly has no purchase on Christians who do not.

Now, so far, I have discussed the version of this argument in its explicit, "Catholic" sense. But I perceive that many Protestants who would never assert this kind of argument nonetheless do believe in a surreptitious version of it. This version presumes that since The Pastor is the Head of the Local Church (as such Christians view ecclesiology), then such a person needs to be male, because only males are to lead.

A feminist critique of this view of church leadership, however, would initially counter that women demonstrably can lead as well as men can. Who seriously doubts, after decades of women leading successfully in virtually every other sector of modern life, that a woman can lead? Who doubts, after decades of women shining in seminary classes and serving successfully in churches, that women can do what contemporary pastors typically do: pray, study, preach, counsel, chair meetings, "cast vision," and so forth? So there seems no reason left to forbid a woman from occupying this role, other than sheer prejudice of the "I'm just not comfortable with a woman as senior pastor" variety.

A feminist critique, moreover, would go on to look at the structure of church leadership itself and wonder, Why is there presumed to be this ecclesiastical hierarchy culminating in One Big Boss? Why is the local church, instead, not led by a council or "college" of shepherds (whether employed full time or part time, or volunteering as they can), each playing different and complementary roles? If we conceive of church leadership this way, wouldn't any such group of pastors be better by including both men and women, who will bring their individual gifts and whatever also inheres in their maleness or femaleness, or masculinity or femininity, to the joint work of shepherding?

I put things this way because I am appealing to the broadest possible audience, and I don't feel I have to take sides in longstanding and complicated arguments about "sex versus gender" or "male/female essence versus the social construction of masculine or feminine identity." These matters are important, to be sure, and we will return to them presently.[10] But I suggest here that *whatever* one's views about them, it simply makes more biblical, theological, and pastoral sense not to put a solitary person on a pastoral pedestal.[11] It makes sense instead to entrust pastoral leadership to a group. And unless we construe leadership in strictly masculine terms—as some, alas, still do—then no matter what we make of male/female or masculine/feminine differences, that group should feature the richest possible array of relevant abilities.[12]

14

Counterarguments from
Church History

History shows us that women emerge in church leadership only in pathological situations—extreme revivalism, schismatic groups, and the rise of cults.

This argument makes sense among Christians who espouse patriarchy as not only divinely ordained, but simply prudent, given women's clear inadequacies and vulnerabilities.[1] It is also a necessary argument for patriarchalists who are obliged to explain the presence of female leaders throughout church history when the Bible, at least to them, seems so clear on the exclusivity of male leadership.

A classic instance of this sort of argument appears in a textbook widely used among evangelicals:

The history of Theosophy then, is marked indelibly by the imprint of the female minds [sic], which, ever since Eve, has apparently been vulnerable to forbidden fruit and the tantalizing tones of various varieties of serpents.

It should be remembered that the Apostle Paul strictly enjoined the Christian Church to forbid women the teaching ministry, especially when men were available to meet this need . . . (I Timothy 2:11-14).

It can be clearly seen from the study of non-Christian cults, ancient and modern, that the female teaching ministry has graphically fulfilled what Paul anticipated in his day by divine revelation, and brought in its wake, as history tells us, confusion, division and strife. This is true from Johanna Southcutt to Mary Baker Eddy to Helena Blavatsky and the Fox sisters, all of whom were living proof of our Lord's declaration that "if the blind lead the blind, both shall fall into the ditch" (Matthew 15:14b).[2]

The immediate response to this nonsense, of course, is simple. If it is true that a few deviant movements have been founded by women, then we might well ask, Who began *all the other* cults—that is, the vast majority of them? That's right—it was non-women. (And, we might ask further, who has been responsible for the vast majority of heresies as well as just the mass of deficient theology taught through the ages within the church? Yes, it's the same class of humans, and it's not women.) Mercifully, no responsible complementarian argues this way anymore.

From the other side of the debate comes the recognition and celebration of women in leadership, even if it was indeed on the margins: those within the Montanist movement; various women's orders in the Middle Ages—perhaps most notably the Beguines; the notorious case of Anne Hutchinson in Puritan New England; female preachers in the eighteenth- and nineteenth-century evangelical revivals; and the prominent women among Pentecostal and charismatic clergy in the twentieth and twenty-first centuries. For some traditional Christians, this checkered heritage "proves" that women are not to lead in mainstream churches. But this is viciously circular logic. If women have not been allowed to lead within mainstream Christianity (although Pentecostal-charismatic Christianity is rapidly becoming the global mainstream), but have found freedom to serve in such ways only in the occasional marginal movement, then female leadership ipso facto will be linked with marginal movements—thus "disqualifying" it from mainstream consideration!

Yet the matter does not stop here. Female leadership is evident even within mainstream movements of various sorts: female abbesses, mystics, and teachers in the Middle Ages, such as Margery Kempe, Julian of Norwich, and Hildegard of Bingen;[3] female evangelists and preachers encouraged by John Wesley, Charles Finney, and Dwight Moody; female pastors trained by such mainstream institutions as Moody Bible Institute at the turn of the twentieth century and ordained by such indubitably orthodox denominations as the Evangelical Free Church (even though such institutions turned against women's ordination in later decades);[4] female missionaries and parachurch leaders from all denominations throughout the "great century" of Protestant missions and beyond;[5] and contemporary women speakers who have commanded considerable audiences as Bible teachers and authors even as their message has been ostensibly a traditional, complementarian one, such as Elisabeth Elliot, Anne Graham Lotz, and Jill Briscoe. These examples can hardly be dismissed as marginal. Indeed, as many historians have pointed out, female preachers and pastors have been a hallmark of evangelicalism in particular (versus liberal, or Roman Catholic, or Orthodox Christianity) from its very inception—with gender lines forming only when the evangelical movement in question "moves uptown" in a quest for acceptance by the broader society.[6]

Nowadays, of course, we also can consider the experience of mainstream Protestant churches throughout the West that have employed women in pastoral and theological leadership for some decades. Will anyone seriously gainsay the effectiveness of their labors? What, indeed, can complementarians make of the evident fruitfulness of women's preaching and pastoral ministries among white, black, Hispanic, Asian, and other congregations in North America, the United Kingdom, Europe, Australia, New Zealand, Africa, Latin America, and Asia? The burgeoning house church movement in China alone is a massive counterexample, led as it is predominately by women. The best answer patriarchalists can give, I suppose, is to say that God still prefers only men to do it, but will settle for the work being done by whoever will do it.

Happily, there is another interpretative option: God works along the general social contours of patriarchal society, taking us as we are, even as the creative and liberating pressure of the Holy Spirit on that society first ameliorates some of the most oppressive aspects of patriarchy and then ultimately opens it up to the full equality of women. The church when it is in the white heat of revival or missionary advance often shows us glimpses of the order of the kingdom of God to come, but the world is not ready for it yet. So these exciting and emancipating movements subside into socially acceptable patriarchy, awaiting the day when such compromise is no longer strategic. That day, I have been arguing, has come in some societies.

Again, I must make it clear that I am not advocating a "realized eschatology," a radical claim that "the Day of the Lord" has already come and come in its fullness. Rather, I am arguing on the basis of the simple observation of the social fact that the recent advocacy of Christian egalitarianism has arisen in the context of the general egalitarianism in modern culture. Therefore, the mainstreaming of women's full dignity in home and church should be a priority with all Christians in such cultures. There is no longer any reason to hold back, and every reason to move forward.

Christian feminism is simply a capitulation to secular feminism—it is a case of sheer worldliness, of conforming to a secular cultural agenda.

The contention from some complementarians that Christian feminists are a pathetic group of wannabes chasing after the bandwagon of secular feminism, desperate to be au courant and politically correct, can be answered in two ways.[7]

First, the charge isn't true. Christian feminism is a hundred years older than the books of Betty Friedan and Gloria Steinem on this side of the Atlantic, and of Simone de Beauvoir on the other. Christian feminism arose in the nineteenth century—in temperance movements, suffragist movements, and, in America in particular, alongside abolitionist movements. So, if the *post hoc ergo propter hoc* fallacy here is to be maintained, one ought to argue (implausibly, to be sure) the other way 'round: that Ms. Friedan and her sisters are the ones who are trying to catch up with the evangelicals.[8]

The second response to the charge that Christian feminism is merely a response to secular feminism is that even if it were true, it wouldn't necessarily be a bad thing. For who cares where a good idea originates? In the providence of God, feminist values of human dignity and human rights have come to be championed by secularists, Jews, and others. Hurrah! Christians should then recognize and rejoice in these developments, even as we have to admit that we have been slower than some others to grasp these values ourselves. Moreover, we ought to recognize that these values have emerged out of the particular matrix of Western civilization that was shaped so deeply by biblical religion—and have emerged only in that matrix. Instead of resisting these values, therefore, we can be humbly grateful for this provocation from some non-Christians, as well as from some of our fellow Christians, to recover forgotten aspects of our own tradition.

As Dietrich Bonhoeffer tirelessly reminded us, Christ is the Lord of the whole world, not just of the church, and he is at work by the Spirit in the whole world, not just in the church.[9] If someone is willing to protect the weak, feed the hungry, free the oppressed, beautify the land, or teach the truth, Christians properly give thanks for that good work to the one true God from whom all blessings flow. Thus Christian feminists can celebrate any sort of feminism that brings more justice and human flourishing to the world—more shalom—no matter who is bringing it, since we recognize the hand of God in all that is good.[10] As Stephen Carter remarks, "Religious conservatives who rail against feminism would do well to consider the centuries of male nonintegrity that gave feminism birth."[11] And we Christians then can contribute to feminism the distinctive insights of the gospel and especially the model of our Lord Jesus, who shows us God's will toward women and men better than does anyone else.

15

Counterarguments from Contemporary Experience and Practice

This kind of argument can be used to support the legitimization of homosexuality.

It is true that certain kinds of feminist arguments can be deployed in the service of defending homosexuality. I do not agree, however, that the paradigm I am offering in this book can be used in this campaign. In short, I contend that the cases of gender and of sexual identity/desire/behavior are not, in fact, parallel.

To be sure, inasmuch as any human being has been treated politically and socially as subhuman, Christians must object. People of various sexual orientations, desires, and practices are our neighbors—indeed, some of them are our fellow Christians—and we must love them as we love ourselves. We thus ought to have been contending for the fundamental human rights of all of our neighbors as hard as we contended for anyone's.

Moreover, one of the key debating points in this larger public question is just what constitutes a "human right" and what instead constitutes social privilege, responsibility, and so on. Robert Benne and Gerald McDermott illustrate this point in regard to the controversy over same-sex marriage:

There are huge differences between constitutional rights with few restrictions (such as the rights to life or free speech) and other rights with important restrictions, which do not carry the right of universal access. We already recognize that not everyone has the right to enlist in the army, but that one must be of the proper age, physical condition, citizenship, and philosophy—anarchists and pacifists need not apply. We also agree that certain persons do not have the right to marriage—children, multiple partners, family members, and those already married.[1]

The argument therefore continues, even in jurisdictions (such as my own country, Canada) in which same-sex marriages are legal, as to what all is included in the package of generic and universal human rights versus privileges, options, requirements, and the like. Christians therefore must continue to work for full justice for all even as we recognize that the debate is far from settled as to just what "full justice" means for those of different sexual preferences—and for everyone else.

There is yet no comfort to be found in my paradigm for Christians pressing for a new acceptance of sexual varieties. For, to reiterate, the cases (sexual orientation/desire/practice versus race or sex) are not parallel in Scripture.

Let's return to the case of slavery, under which I will subsume racism (since race was the basis for slavery in Canada and the United States and thus frames the discourse here), a case on which I can assume all readers of this book will agree. As we have seen, slavery was, at best, condoned in Scripture: patriarchs owned slaves in the Old Testament, and Christians owned slaves in the New without clear divine disapproval. Yet four other facts must be noticed as well: (1) slavery is never commanded by God, never normalized in any explicit way in the Bible; (2) slavery is ameliorated significantly in the Old Testament in comparison with the practices of nations surrounding Israel; (3) slaves are described in both Testaments, in fact, to be the human equals of their masters, fully bearing the image of God; and (4) the egalitarianism of the New Testament community of believers (Gal 3:28 etc., and especially Paul's epistle to Philemon) stretches slavery to the breaking point of incoherence. Paul all but says, "It just doesn't make sense, Philemon, for you to employ your Christian brother Onesimus as a slave, so—"

When it comes to gender in the Bible, we have a case that is generally similar to that of slavery. Patriarchy is practiced and condoned in both Testaments as well. The main difference with the case of slavery is that in the New Testament male leadership is explicitly taught for both home and church, and Jesus and the apostles themselves seem to observe certain gender lines (e.g., all twelve apostles are male; Paul teaches silence and submission to women), while none of them were involved in slaveholding. Still, (2) and (3) remain the same: patriarchy is ameliorated significantly in both Testaments vis-à-vis the surrounding cultures, and women are regarded as equal with men in respect to their full humanity. When it comes to (4), we have even more evidence of patriarchy being something other than God's ideal but instead a feature of the social landscape with which God works. As I have detailed in chapter eleven, there is a "doubleness" in the Bible's regard for and depiction of women and their roles that, in my view, can be understood consistently only in terms of the eventual and total emancipation of women as truly, fully equal.

In both of these cases, then, the Bible presents a pattern that supports and ameliorates both the temporary, culture-specific accommodation of slavery and patriarchy, on the one hand, and also the principles that not only support, but even compel, the causes of abolitionism and feminism, on the other.

There is no such "doubleness" pattern, however, regarding sexual diversity.[2] The Bible instead is univocal, from cover to cover, on the matter of sexual intercourse: the only legitimate and healthy pattern is heterosexual, adult, and exclusive within the covenant of marriage. Not only is homoerotic sex ruled out, but so is every other form of sexual intercourse outside this pattern.[3]

Indeed, resistance to the religious redefinition of marriage to include same-sex unions—whatever the state decides to do about such things—is a matter on which egalitarians and complementarians can and should agree.[4] Christians recognize that, from Genesis 2 onward, the Bible assumes that there is something crucially complementary about the marriage of a man and a woman (versus *same*-sex unions), just as God created humanity in his image as "male and female" in Genesis 1. I immediately acknowledge that our current cultural wisdom and social science comes nowhere close to defining precisely and to everyone's satisfaction in what that complementarity consists. To put it mildly, there is no "essential" definition of "man" and "woman" that commands the field. (Indeed, many feminists continue to fear any such "essentialism" entirely as a tool for the continuing denigration of women and confinement of them in predetermined roles.)[5] But the biblical pattern implies that there *is* something crucially complementary to this union of one man and one woman that no other form of union (not polygamy or polyandry, not homosexuality, not serial marriages) can instantiate or duplicate properly and thus constitute a proper marriage. Marriage, after all, is not just about procreation, but about companionship (Gen 2) in the work of gardening the earth and fulfilling the cultural mandate (Gen 1). And this companionable union is intrinsically tied to the male and female spouses being at once similar and different, as the powerful imagery of Genesis 2 shows, and as the subsequent uniform biblical pattern maintains.

More particularly, the biblical proscription of homosexual intercourse is not arbitrary. The Bible presents homosexual intercourse as the mark of psychospiritual pathology—whatever its origin might be in nature, nurture, or some combination of the two. Investigation into the origin of such sexual desires might well be helpful in terms of awareness, therapy, and mutual understanding and respect. But the question of etiology is importantly beside the *moral* point. The origin of *anyone's* psychological and spiritual problems—whether inclinations to pride, alcoholism, promiscuity, self-loathing, self-righteousness, or violence—is not the central issue in the Bible. What is foremost is the proper *response* to our deficits and disorders.[6] Those who identify LGBTQ desires in themselves must therefore, if they are Christians, faithfully submit to whatever restrictions are appropriate to the character of their problems—just as those who prefer to be promiscuous must nonetheless be chaste, pedophiles must nonetheless avoid dangerous situations with children, and the self-righteous must nonetheless practice charity and humility toward even the subjects of their condemnation.[7]

The fundamental point here is that nowhere in the Bible is there anything *culpable* about *being* a woman *who happens to have to live in a patriarchal situation* or *being* a person *who happens to have to live in an enslaved situation*. Nor is there anything wrong, therefore, with *acting* in a way consonant with that situation. Indeed, the evil in the situation would consist instead in whatever subordination one is experiencing when nothing about one's nature in fact justifies such treatment. Contrarily, the Bible explicitly condemns the *actions* involved in homosexual intercourse as *sins*, deriving them from what the Bible sees to be disordered human passions (Rom 1). The whole categorization of so-called homosexuals in the Bible (and I recognize that the term itself is a modern construct and subject to various forms of critique) is in terms of *wrong actions* stemming from *wrongly oriented sexual desires*.

The only parallel I can see, then, is the important parallel of human rights: treating everyone, whatever their sin, as fellow-sinning-human-beings-who-nonetheless-bear-the-image-of-God. Again, please hear me when I agree that we Christians have a lot of ground to make up in advocating for the just treatment of those with LGBTQ desires. What is decidedly *not* parallel in Scripture, however, is the moral status of slaves and women versus those who choose to engage in sexual actions not sanctioned by God. And let's also be clear that in the latter category are not only those unusual forms of sexual desire that the Bible feels obliged to condemn only once in a while, because relatively few people are inclined to them—whether homosexual, bestial, incestual, or necrophiliac—but also plain old heterosexual fornication and adultery, which the Bible spends quite a bit of time depicting and denouncing since many of us are strongly inclined to them.

So much, then, for the tiresomely repeated argument that "the Bible says very little about homosexuality and says a lot instead about, say, self-righteousness, or caring for the poor, or. . . ." First, the Bible says very little about matters about which it can normally be safely assumed not much needs to be said. The Bible doesn't tell us to keep breathing, for example, or to make sure to ingest enough water every day. It doesn't tell us not to stick our heads into the mouths of lions. And in cases in which a relatively small number of people are inclined to do what normally people don't do, and in such cases in which such actions would have serious consequences (as opposed to, say, a harmless, if eccentric, hobby), and in such cases in which normal human traditions cannot be counted on to provide this wisdom (as they do in the case of avoiding predators), the Bible does speak: sharply, categorically, and briefly—as is exactly the case with sexual deviations. On subjects on which the majority of Bible readers seem to need regular reminding, however, the Bible regularly reminds: caring for the poor, indeed, along with worshiping the one true God, guarding against sin, choosing the path of life-giving discipline, and so on.

Second, the fact that the Bible says that A is more important than B doesn't mean that B therefore should be understood as unimportant. Yet over and over one reads people arguing this fallacious way: "What *really* matters is A, so let's not fight over B." The question of contending over B has nothing to do with the higher importance of A, but with whether B is argument-worthy. (The exception here would be if fighting over B somehow entailed our neglecting A. But unless that zero-sum situation can be demonstrated as actually occurring, the debate over B stands on its own ground as however important it actually is.) So yes, of course, some things matter more than sexual relations. But not many seem to matter more than that—in any culture. And just because, say, worship of God or caring for the poor matters more doesn't mean that everything that matters less than those fundamental issues doesn't matter at all, or can be safely left to individual preference.

This small book is not about sexual varieties, of course, so I cannot and should not try to develop a full discussion of that subject here. Given the cultural climate, however, in which many people— including an increasing number even of evangelical Christians—are in fact arguing that a consistent advocacy for feminism entails a similar defense of the legitimacy of the range of desires and behaviors symbolized by "LGBTQ," I have to indicate why I think there is no strong parallel between the biblical defense of feminism and the latter agenda.[8]

Now, the two arguments that give me the most pause in dealing with gender do not stem from biblical, theological, or historical grounds. I'm convinced that the model I have presented is the best of those I have encountered so far. But I do want to heed two warnings, the first from complementarians and the second from feminists, that challenge the practical implications of this model.

If women don't stay home, children will be neglected.

A decade ago, *The Atlantic* magazine featured a cover story on how white, middle-class, feminist women have been able to realize their dream of entering the workplace while also having children. They have done so, the article suggests, only by the expedient of hiring other women to care for those children and help with the housework—the female share of which has not diminished in many households, despite protestations from men about how enlightened they are about feminism. Indeed, as one wag has put it, "Feminism means that women now have to look after the car, too." The Supermom cannot, in fact, do it all or have it all. So in this scenario, children are not neglected, but they are being raised by caregivers who are not their parents.[9] Since then, women have been encouraged to "Lean In" to their possibilities—which possibilities are dramatically expanded, of course, if one has a husband who loves being with the kids and has a flexible schedule he is willing to exploit to cover for his wife's various pursuits and obligations, and has a household income such that most domestic chores are handled by personal assistants, maids, gardeners, and the like.[10]

Further down the economic ladder, however, are the many more working mothers who are not "realizing" any "dream," but working because they have to. Either they are single—as many, many mothers now are in North America—or the cost of living is such that they must join their husbands in the work force. And their children have to be placed in one or another sort of daycare that is often of dubious quality. Thus there is a weird and widespread handing over of children from richer to poorer down a chain of wealth.

Caring for children while staying afloat economically is a genuine challenge for most, and a dreadful challenge for many. (It also is hardly a new challenge: a century ago, women's magazines were wrestling with "the woman's dilemma" of managing both home and job.[11]) Simply preaching a return to the "traditional family" is no answer. In fact, it is offensively obtuse. This sort of family is actually not found in the Bible anyway, or in most of the history of the church. The ideal family touted by so many North American evangelical preachers is an artifact of a very particular era: the post–World War II boom in which a man could earn a household's worth of income even on an assembly line, and everyone else could stay home or in school. Such a family now has almost vanished from the economic landscape largely *for economic reasons.*

Some have argued in response that these wages have disappeared because women have entered the work force, and thus employers can lower wages in the face of a greater supply of workers. Thus feminism is to blame. I am no economist, but obviously there are other huge factors at stake. Increased mechanization facilitated by computers has replaced many industrial and clerical jobs. Globalization, facilitated by lower-cost long-distance transportation, changed tariffs, and improved telecommunications, has resulted in many jobs being moved offshore.[12] And women have indeed entered the workforce in greater numbers, but many have been escaping abusive marriages via liberalized divorce laws and have had to find paid employment to support themselves and their children.

Wherever the blame lies—if "blame" is even a useful concept in matters of economic and social evolution—the traditionalist attempt to turn back the clock will not help. There is no point in calling everyone to move back to Levittown and *Leave It to Beaver*. And it is simply absurd, as well as insulting, to suggest that these various and complex social ills would be cured if we would just put men back in charge and women back in the kitchen.

Feminism can help here by reframing the challenge for each family. Instead of various tasks and responsibilities being characterized as "women's work" or "men's work," there is just *work*, and *we* have to get it done somehow. So what are *we* going to do? If it turns out that many more women than men prefer to tend the home and care for the children most of the time—whether from nature or nurture (who knows?)—then so be it. Those families are *choosing together* what to do, not *automatically* relegating the woman to the domestic sphere and the man to the marketplace. Thus also those unusual families in which the woman goes out to work and the man stays home. (I have one set of relatives who have followed this pattern at times, and our youngest son has had excellent before- and after-school care from a man in a family such as this.) Such families are free to practice this pattern without emasculating the man or defeminizing the woman. And any intermediate arrangement, such as many families now practice (often one or both spouses working less than full time and sharing in various domestic duties), also should enjoy the same legitimacy. The liberty here is to do whatever makes the most of the particular gifts, desires, opportunities, and needs of the individuals that make up that family, without simplistically sorting things according to sex.

Or does anyone still want to argue seriously that all women, everywhere and always, are much more suited to domestic duties, and all men, everywhere and always, are much more suited to the workplace? Again, social science demonstrates what we all now know from our own experience: such universal generalizations just aren't true of every person or couple, so we need a paradigm that includes and guides everyone, not just most.[13] In the next section, I will address further the question of defining masculinity and femininity in family and church along these lines.

If this paradigm of gender is to be accepted, then the church should still not only tolerate, but comply with, patriarchy today in the many parts of the world that still practice it—and that is repugnant.

One critical *feminist* response to the paradigm I present in this book would be that this proposal is, in fact, tolerant of the oppression of women and therefore tolerant of sin. Indeed, this paradigm would encourage Christians to perpetuate patriarchal structures even today in those parts of the world in which society is not prepared to embrace full equality for women. Even worse, from a feminist point of view, is the sin of ascribing such a policy of tolerance toward patriarchy to the very will of God, as if the Holy One can not only look on sin but also put up with it indefinitely—and even work through it.

I take this charge seriously. As a feminist myself (albeit a white, privileged, male feminist), I abhor the idea of contributing the slightest legitimacy to the perpetuation of patriarchy. As a Christian, furthermore, I *hate* the notion that I would ascribe to God something unworthy of him—indeed, something evil.

As I look hard at the Bible, however, and at the two thousand years of church history since the Bible's completion, it seems that God has in fact accommodated himself over and over to the weakness and even the sin of human beings. He also has called his faithful ones to a similar accommodation. The "already, but not yet" tension—the situation in which the light of God's Word and kingdom breaks into our situation truly, but not fully—is clear not only in the coming of Christ, but throughout the Old Testament story of redemption as well. God chooses a people as a vehicle for global salvation, and then works with them in a convoluted trajectory of obedience and blessing, disobedience and punishment, first this way and then that way. God puts up with a compromised plan for the conquest of Canaan, blesses a monarchy he didn't want, forestalls for generations the judgment his own prophets foretold on both northern and southern kingdoms, and even then preserves a remnant and reestablishes them in Jerusalem. God works not only through Israel, for all its wickedness, but also through the evil empires of Egypt, Assyria, Babylon, Persia, and Rome. God works not only through prophets and saints but through Joseph's vindictive brothers, resentful Balaam (and his donkey), and rulers as ruthless as Nebuchadnezzar and Darius, Caiaphas and Pilate.

Much more needs to be said on this matter.[14] It remains evident in Scripture and history, however, that God does in fact "draw straight with crooked lines" on the tortured topography of the troubled creation he loves and is redeeming. He works with what he's got. He doesn't fix everything at once, but presses as hard as he can—that is, as hard as the situation itself will bear, and with primary values preferred over secondary or tertiary ones—to maximize shalom in every situation, even as *no* situation perfectly realizes his perfect values. And God calls his people to do the same.

This paradigm I am offering here, however, should not be construed as a call merely to acquiesce to patriarchy. Much less is it a blessing on it. Patriarchy is, I say again, a result of the fall. As Cornelius Plantinga suggests about sin in general, patriarchy particularly is "not the way it's supposed to be."[15] Instead, the paradigm I offer here echoes the fundamental biblical call to work for shalom, for the full flourishing of every woman and every man, every slave and every master, every child and every parent, as God gives us opportunity to do so.

Where and when God does *not* give us opportunity to do so, we pray that he will soon. And in the meanwhile—that is a crucial phrase in this paradigm, *in the meanwhile*—we trust him to work his good will in and through us, whatever be the structures with which we temporarily must comply. Thus we will indeed have to comply with patriarchy, just as we (like the apostles) will have to comply with corrupt governments, or with exploitative businesses, or with hypocritical charities, or with dysfunctional families. No institution or society remains untouched by evil in this world, and in fact we are all deeply infected and affected by it. *In the meanwhile*, we live as the patriarchs lived, as the prophets lived, as the apostles lived, and as saints—women and men—in every age have lived. We live with hope in God that one day all of this tension, compromise, and accommodation to human sin will be done away with. And we live with the sure sense that God is right here with us, comforting us in our oppression, forgiving us our own sins—even sins of complicity with evil—grieving with us that things have to be this way for now, and empowering us nonetheless to bring gospel light to the darkest corners of the earth.

I do not enjoy advancing this idea. I am sure, however, it was much more difficult for dedicated Christian feminist Gretchen Gaebelein Hull to make this same point some decades ago as she addressed her sisters in Christ with the following poignant plea:

> Can *you* drink the cup of submission? Yes, I realize full well what many of you are thinking: *That's all we've ever done.* But I would ask of you: Can you now drink the cup as Christ means you to drink it? Not because you must, but because you choose to? Would you be willing to put aside your legitimate rights, if the time to exercise them is not yet right in your particular circumstances? Would you be willing to put your career on hold, if that is in the best interests of your family or your cultural milieu? Will you work for change in a patient and loving manner, rather than sinking into anger or bitterness? Will you commit yourself to work in a Christ-like way, even if you are in un-Christ-like situations?[16]

It perhaps will help clarify this point to acknowledge that the argument I am setting out in this book would apply—in part—to the terribly vexing problem faced by Christians today in many parts of Africa, namely, polygamy. As thousands, even millions, are converting to Christianity, Christian leaders properly call them to Christian morality, which includes Christian marriage of just one man and one woman. In many of the social contexts in which these converts must continue to live, however, for a man to set aside every wife but his first, and to disown all children from subsequent marriages, would be to surrender them to disaster. Women have so little opportunity to make a living on their own—beyond prostitution and other horrific occupations—that Christian leaders feel caught in a clash of Christian values.

Applying my paradigm to this situation would involve recognizing polygamy—as it appears in the Old Testament just as it appears today in Africa—as an accommodation to deep social problems, and as itself a social problem, certainly not as God's ideal. (As I have already pointed out, one cannot find a happy polygamous home anywhere in the Old Testament.) Thus Christian leaders have condoned polygamy immediately where it seems the most helpful way *for women and children*—for the "little ones" who are the oppressed in these social structures. As they do so, however, they simultaneously teach the *better way* of Christian monogamy and work for the transformation of society such that polygamy can be eliminated as soon as possible.

The parallel with my suggestion regarding patriarchy is only partial, however. For polygamy can be seen as the "best of available options" for the women themselves in certain societies. So why should we tolerate patriarchy when it is *not* the best option for women? We should do so only because the only other course—resistance to patriarchy—would somehow harm the cause of the gospel, perhaps by embittering people against Christianity and with little or no prospect of actually helping change the status of women (as was the case in first-century churches). I think of a brilliant alumna who serves as a missionary with her husband in a Muslim-majority nation. She is every bit the feminist I am, but she sits in the back seat of their car, veils her head, walks behind her husband and in all other respects—"stupid, but trivial, respects," she calls them—conforms with the patriarchal customs of that culture in order to focus her neighbors' attention on their sharing of Jesus and the gospel, and not on disruptive Christian views of gender equality. "First things first," she says.

This attitude, then, represents a form of Christian realism that seeks the advance of the gospel above all other values with a clear-eyed recognition of what can and cannot be done in any given situation. Thus (and I say this carefully) polygamy itself would be tolerated even if it were *not* better for women—as slavery certainly wasn't better for slaves—if the higher gospel priorities were at stake.[17]

This is a "hard saying" indeed. But it must be understood alongside the affirmation that any compliance with patriarchy ought to be undertaken only with grief over its evil and with a determination to ameliorate it as quickly and as extensively as possible. Furthermore, we Christians must keep the pressure on our society to keep changing its ways for the better in terms of gender as on all other fronts of shalom-making—including pressing our own families and churches to change.

And for once in this book I write as a man to men: we generally still have more power than women, and we must seek to use it on their behalf in a way that is appropriate to our context. In most cases in North American society today, that context means that men must join women in the vanguard of Christian feminism—in our homes, churches, and beyond. These issues are not "women's issues" but *human* issues. This set of concerns is a key opportunity for us men to advocate for "the other." Striving for the full equality of women is what it means to love women as we love ourselves.

To be sure, we Christians are not God's only agents of change—neither as individuals nor as the church. And we must beware Christian talk that suggests that we *are* God's only agent of change—as if nothing will happen if we don't do it. God is himself the primary agent of all good change, and he works through all the means available to him, including individuals and institutions that do not praise him and yet must accomplish his providential will. Both the Bible and world history show us that God works in mysterious ways, and through many unexpected channels, to achieve his purposes.

Let us do our part, then, with vigor, creativity, perseverance, hope, and humility before the sovereign agenda of God. Let us press in every situation to see whether there is here a God-given opportunity to increase shalom.[18] But where it is evidently not time for this idea or practice to yield, we must not resort to revolutionary violence that will impede a society's reception of the gospel, and especially if it will not yield any actual benefit to the oppressed. Throwing ourselves into the teeth of cultural reality on misguided missions is worse than useless: it can stiffen resistance. And I trust it is clear that this principle can apply also to small societies such as individual families and congregations. Again, if the family or church in question is not in fact ripe for change, forcing the issue will result only in damage to the measure of shalom already achieved in that society, and may well set back the momentum of positive change God has been establishing.

Some women and men will feel that they must leave recalcitrant churches for freer ministry elsewhere, and many should do so with a clear conscience. They may well be wasting their time and talent in a situation devoid of any prospect of significant change and could minister more fruitfully in another context. But many of us cannot, or ought not to, leave such churches—nor can we leave our families or national societies. So if we stay, we ought to promote gospel priorities as best we can, stay alert for any new openings, trust God for strength for the day, and yearn for that Dawn when all such compromises will be rendered unnecessary.

16

What Then?

GUIDING PRINCIPLES

As we seek to respond properly to a social situation involving patri-archy—whether a marriage or a church, in the instances discussed in this book—there are a number of principles that can guide us: ac-tivism, realism, vocation, and hope.

Activism. "Blessed are the peacemakers," preached Jesus, and we should make all of the shalom that we can. In particular, we should further the flourishing of human society by the fullest possible par-ticipation of women and men, without prejudice or constraint. We cannot *perfect* our marriages, churches, or larger societies, but we are not called to do so. We are, instead, called to do what we can to extend the kingdom of God. So if we get any chance to improve a marriage or a church, we should.

Realism. Jesus told us to love God and to love our neighbors. But we need to see as clearly as we can what it means to love God and our neighbors in a given situation. Given a particular set of circumstances, what does God want to happen? Given what the limitations seem to be, what are God's priorities? Given who the neighbors are in this case, in what ways can I love them, and in what ways will they let me do so? Such realism will help us make the necessary hard decisions in a world in which we typically cannot succeed in everything we attempt, a world in which we frequently have to settle for half a loaf, a world in which we often confront a conflict of values and have to work for the higher at the cost of the lower.

Vocation. God calls us all to come to Christ, follow him, and grow up to maturity in him. He calls the church to work with him in his great mission of drawing the world back to himself. He also calls us individually to our particular forms of service, according to the gifts, limitations, and circumstances of our particular lives. We cannot do everything, and we are not called to try to do everything. We need instead to see where God best put us to work, leaving all that we are *not* equipped or positioned to do in God's hands.

Hope. God gives us immediate hope that our current labor, however vexed by suffering, will produce lasting results as it is validated and assisted by him. God also gives us the great final hope that soon our suffering will cease, that injustice will be terminated, and that Christ will return to establish his kingdom of lasting shalom.

How, then, can these principles apply to particular sets of challenges and opportunities?

Fundamentally, we need to do what we can to improve this marriage or family, and this fellowship of Christians. If nothing can be done today, then we stay alert to what can be done tomorrow. In the meanwhile, we imitate the pattern of Jesus as best we can in all we do, and especially in our domestic and ecclesial relationships. We build relationships of love by loving according to how we *can* love in the situation. And those relationships are then in place to support changes that can be sought in a changed situation. Still, usually something *can* be done now, so let's look around and see what can be improved. Some marriages and churches are ripe for significant change, even a wholesale change of paradigm, and I hope that this book will encourage and facilitate such change.

We also need to consider once more, however, just what a particular individual or a particular group or class of people can accomplish in a given situation. Many young people, for example, will not be heard by their elders in a particular church, no matter how right they are. And many women will not be heard by many men—or even by other women. Such marginalizing is not fair, and it's not good, but it's sometimes the way it is. Christians in such contexts must jettison any illusion that they will be heard simply on the merits of their arguments and regardless of the social realities of the situation. That is just not the way human beings process things. They then need to decide among their *actual* options how they can best honor God and advance his kingdom.

Lest I be misheard on this point, let me affirm my belief that, yes, the Holy Spirit can transform hearts, even suddenly, and the Spirit does so sometimes in surprising ways. But we need to see realistically that what we're talking about now is a suspension of normal human relations. It is what I call a sociological or psychological *miracle*. And if we don't have strong grounds to expect such a miracle in a given instance, then we should make our choices along the lines of the norms of everyday life—before we become not only bitter at our fellow church members for their stubbornness, but bitter at God for not performing the miracle we sought.

The principle of realism further reminds us that there are some situations in which pushing feminism too fast and too far will cause rupture and even destruction of a marriage or a congregation. And that seems, at least generally, not to be God's will. The ideologue may draw personal satisfaction from his or her purity and zeal. But—to put the matter starkly—God cares about actual people much more than he does about abstract principles, he wants the maximum amount of shalom to be produced and is willing to wait for it, and he knows how fast and how far human beings can change. God has shown that he will bring us along patiently, as fast as we can go—but only as fast as we can go. So in some circumstances the policy needs to be slow, steady pressure on a marriage or a church to change, with appreciative cooperation with all of the genuine work the Spirit is doing therein. We must be careful not to run ahead of the Spirit of God.

Perhaps in a given church, sadly, it is best that those convinced of egalitarianism finally take leave of those who are not so convinced. The result can be two churches functioning in integrity, rather than one that seethes with resentment and conflict to the cost of the gospel's spread. And, as I have already allowed, the kingdom of God might well be better advanced by an individual withdrawing from a given body and joining another church. Such a person will not be impeded in his or her ministry, and his or her former church will not be impeded in its vocation by spending energy contending with the outlier.

In the case of a marriage, divorce would be an option only if the patriarchal treatment of the wife is severe enough. What counts as "severe enough" would have to be assessed in context, of course. God loves us all and grieves over anyone's suffering. He also particularly cares for the vulnerable and oppressed. But it remains true also that God sometimes calls us to difficult relationships, and we are not to leave just any unpleasant situation. This is genuine Christian liberty: to use our freedom for God, our neighbor, and ourselves.

Someone suffering abuse, I should make plain, should free herself or himself from it if she or he possibly can. No proper Christian teaching about suffering in general, or about voluntary subordination within marriage or church, can bless abuse by telling people to stay in such situations if they can escape them. We especially must guard against the tolerance of abuse "for the sake of the church's reputation" or "for the sake of the pastor's reputation"—for abuse happens in Christian and even clerical homes as well, and it must be rooted out there as it must be rooted out everywhere else.[1]

We live in a culture, however, in which many people leave churches and marriages as freely as they leave jobs and clubs when they encounter a little genuine hardship, or even mere disappointment. So the ethical tension here is inescapable. We can counsel neither to "stick it out at all costs" nor "leave whenever you like." We must recall God's priorities and sort things through as carefully as we can—ideally with the help of Christian sisters and brothers who can share their wisdom and provide practical support.

Finally, I want to affirm the principle of vocation in this sense: God calls different people to different kinds of activism. Some situations need firebrands to provoke the rest of us to the ideas and actions we ought to have thought and done on our own. Some situations need mediators to help make temperate and edifying communication possible. Some situations need friendly people who work hard at maintaining good relations across ideological divides. Some situations need patient folk who go about their kingdom business and just put up with whatever afflictions come their way.

These different sorts of people can annoy each other during a controversy. The activists can't understand the friendly people fraternizing with the enemy. The mediators wish the activists wouldn't keep setting fires for the mediators to put out. And the patient folk often don't see what all the fuss is about and sometimes question the motives and usefulness of all this activity.

So let us appreciate that some situations need *all* of these people at the *same* time, each contributing according to their gifts, limitations, and opportunities. And let us, each and all, seek to love God and love our neighbors as best we can, while supporting other people following their callings in their own, different ways. This is how the kingdom of God has advanced, and will advance, to the final benefit of all women and men and to the glory of the God who loves us so much.

AND NOW, YOUR TURN . . .

Such qualified conclusions cannot sit easily with any feminist. And I doubt that I have now convinced every complementarian reader! But may I say again that the theological challenge before any of us is not to solve every difficulty perfectly—nor is it to convince everyone else. The theological challenge for me, and for you, and for all of us in our churches is to ask God to help us select the best option among those available. I believe that this model of gender equality takes seriously the concerns, arguments, and strengths of both sides. I also think it compensates for at least some of the weaknesses of both sides. I understand it to square well with the eschatological tension in which we really live: already, but not yet. I have concluded that it matches up best with the pattern of God's actual activity in the Bible, as well as with the Bible's particular teachings about gender. And I affirm that this model has been evident in the history of the church.

I do not pretend, however, to have solved every exegetical, theological, historical or practical problem even to my own satisfaction, much less anyone else's. Thus I recall Paul's good advice: "Each of us will be accountable to God. Let us therefore no longer pass judgment on one another, but resolve instead never to put a stumbling block or hindrance in the way of another" (Rom 14:12-13).

I ask, then, that you will forgive me if any of this book has been a stumbling block or hindrance to you. Just set it aside if it has. There has been too much antagonism, even violence, in this debate. My prayer instead has been to follow the scriptural injunction: "Let us consider how to provoke one another to love and good deeds" (Heb 10:24). If you have been provoked, I pray God that he and you will channel that provocation into positive reflection and spiritual fruit from which many women and men will benefit, to the glory of his name.

Let's be clear with ourselves, and with each other, that no one makes up his or her mind about such a set of crucial issues simply on the basis of theological argument. We dare not flatter ourselves that we sit on some intellectual height, calmly weighing each item in the balance of our finely calibrated intellects and entirely sanctified souls.

We are all thoroughly invested in a particular set of assumptions about gender, whatever that set may be. We are all enmeshed in social structures that reward or punish us because of our sex, and because of our views of gender. We simply cannot be disinterested as we decide about this huge, and hugely important, set of issues. So let us own up to those facts. And let us ask ourselves these questions:

What do I really *want* to believe about gender?

Why do I want to believe that?[2]

In particular, what do I think I have to gain or lose by coming to this or that conclusion?

What are the voices in my head telling me to decide on one or another alternative, why would each be telling me that, and how do I feel about each one?

And then we can ask these questions in response:

What shall I do to compensate for my own predispositions, limitations, and desires in order to hear the voice of God as clearly, and searchingly, and transformationally as possible? Am I not only tolerating, but actually seeking out, people who are not just like me, who can be expected to see things differently, and who therefore can offer me information and perspectives I could not have on my own? Am I rigorously comparing the strengths and weaknesses of two or more competing paradigms, honestly attempting to see whether one is superior to the other? Am I listening to the personal testimonies of people who feel that one or another paradigm has damaged them, such that I keep remembering that decisions in these matters have real-world consequences?

Or am I content to just snipe at opponents' arguments, wave away those who would complain about the painful implications of my views, and maintain my current opinion at all costs?

We will make no progress on this question if we do not open our hearts, as well as our minds, to the Spirit of God, in the good company of fellow Christians, with the attitude of submission to whatever God will say to us. The cross stands over us here, as it does everywhere.

We simply must follow the example of young Samuel: "Speak, for your servant is listening" (1 Sam 3:10).

And of young Mary: "Here am I, the servant of the Lord; let it be with me according to your word" (Lk 1:38).

17

Inclusive Language

TOWARD THE END OF THE 1990S, I made a professional move from teaching in the religion department of a mid-sized secular university to a small evangelical theological graduate school. Within a short time of arriving in the latter place, I became aware, to my increasing dismay, of how many of our students were simply unaware of the previous three decades of scholarship defending Christian egalitarianism. Worse, even some of the younger professors we interviewed over the next decade as candidates for teaching positions seemed simply unacquainted with the many arguments offered on behalf of biblical feminism.

I felt as if I had entered a time warp. I had come to Regent from the University of Manitoba expecting to take for granted this painstaking work—undertaken often at considerable personal and professional cost by the scholars involved, many of whom lost their jobs and countless friendships over resistance to their findings—in order to move onward and outward to explore the interesting implications for Christian life of gender-sensitive scholarship in particular and feminist concerns more generally. Instead, I was back to square one, introducing to students the novel and even shocking proposals that women could preach, let alone pastor churches, and that maybe it was not a timeless principle that wives were to defer to their husbands in everything.[1]

My first book on gender, *Finally Feminist*, presented to a broader audience that case I was making to my students. In this new book, I have tried to improve that case. But I now want to go on to discuss a range of issues that take that case as prologue to help us as Christians, and as Anglosphere evangelical Christians in particular, move on to other considerations relevant to a gender-sensitive outlook. I hope hereby to stimulate readers to consider how useful gender-based analysis can be to a wide range of basic issues in Christian living.

Family and church will continue to be key sites for our consideration, both because they are crucial to Christian life and because they are the two social zones over which Christians can exercise the most control, and thus can be aimed at the fullest faithfulness to Christian ideals. Family and church also continue to be the chief zones of resistance to the gender equality for which I am arguing, particularly in the case of what I call the "New Machismo" being offered by popular pastors and authors as the solution to the ostensible problem of the lack of male interest in churchgoing. So we need to keep looking at how best to understand women and men, femaleness and maleness, and femininity and masculinity in those contexts. But I will also trace out at least a few implications of this way of looking at gender into vexed questions in the marketplace, and especially questions of women in organizational leadership positions beyond the church.

Revising our language about an issue is key to our revising our approach to it. The ancient Chinese sage Kong-zi (whom Westerners typically call Confucius) averred strongly that the key initial step in any philosophical consideration—and in any political revision as well—is "the rectification of names." The civil rights struggle in the United States has been marked by the ruling out of certain words as intrinsically demeaning and the substitution of other words as imparting dignity instead. Likewise, mid-twentieth-century feminists successfully pressed for changes in standard English usage in at least two key respects. First, male terms, which had traditionally been used to refer both particularly to men and generally to all human beings, were restricted to the former usage only. "Man" was replaced by "humanity," "his" by "his or hers," and so on. Inclusive language is now required by all standard style guides as simply correct (= conventional) English. Second, the titles "Miss" and "Mrs." were largely, if not universally, replaced by the single title "Ms.," a pseudo-abbreviation (for it corresponded to no longer noun) that was simply meant as a female counterpart to "Mr." No longer, that is, would a woman be characterized immediately by her marital status as if that were the most important thing to know about a woman on encountering her.

Such changes set off alarms particularly among American evangelicals, who worried about the revision of gender norms among human beings, yes, but also about any possible revolution in the way God was understood in gendered terms.[2]

The main site of controversy became Bible translations, a sizable industry among evangelicals. To what extent, if at all, should contemporary Bible translations reflect "inclusive" language for human beings? And then to what extent, if at all, should the Bible's language be revised to correspond to modern gender sensibilities in terms of God?

Many evangelical Christians live in a very strange world. It's a sort of dark Alice-in-Wonderland landscape in which peaceful places can metamorphose hazardously at a moment's notice. At times, the landscape is fairly flat and stable. Lots of different people and communities and ideas and concerns can exist together, with good-natured exchanges all around, including even the occasional sincere and civil disagreement. It's a sort of Serengeti waterhole of inclusivity. But sometimes the ground shifts abruptly, and traditional believers see themselves suddenly perched on top of a steep mountain of truth. From here, any step in any direction is a step down. Worse, any step risks a calamitous slide all the way down a slippery slope to wreckage at the other extreme. Such an earthquake has ruptured the green pastures of Bible translations.

In recent decades, Christians have produced a wide range of versions of the Scriptures they love. Yes, some of us have grumbled, "This one is too wooden" or "That one is too idiosyncratic." And a colorful minority have entertained or bemused the rest of us with their de-

fense of the King James Version (KJV) as if it were divinely inspired—
ironically, in an argument not unlike conservative Roman Catholic
defenses of Jerome's fourth-century Latin translation of Scripture, the
Vulgate, that now enjoys the status of "inspired text" in Catholic tradition. But most Christians tolerate and many even rejoice in the
diversity of translations.

At times, however, resistance to a translation has been intense.
Most significant and widespread among Protestants was the criticism
of the Revised Standard Version (RSV) when it was issued in the 1950s.
Many Christians thought that this translation manifested an ominous
theological agenda: a *liberal* agenda, in fact, that challenged the proper
interpretation of such key doctrines as the virgin birth (so Is 7:14 and
the translation "a young woman" instead of "a virgin") and the
atonement (so 1 Jn 2:2 and 4:10 and the milder word "expiation" sub-
stituted for the King James Version's "propitiation"). Other Christians,
however, were not convinced that the RSV was unfaithful to the Greek
and Hebrew texts, and so used it as a helpful alternative to the ar-
chaic—and therefore often *more* misleading—English expressions of
the KJV.

More recently, however, North American Protestantism has been
wracked with controversy over a quite different issue. Now the
question is so-called inclusive language translations, those versions
that have changed some or all of the Bible's use of generic masculine
language to language that explicitly includes, or at least does not implicitly exclude, women. No more "mankind" or "man" or "he who
will . . ." and so on when all persons, not just males, are meant.

Interestingly, when the New Revised Standard Version (NRSV) was
released in 1989, many Christians, including some evangelicals, were
happy to use it as the first translation to apply such principles in a
sweeping way. Most conservative Christians, however, simply ignored
it. The earlier battle over the RSV perhaps had sorted things out: you
either liked and used the RSV, or you didn't—and the same would go
for the NRSV.

The ground did not heave up until evangelicalism's most widely used modern translation, the New International Version, emerged as a significantly altered edition in 1995. Periodicals such as *World* magazine, Bible scholars such as the complementarian Wayne Grudem, and popular leaders such as Focus on the Family's James Dobson sounded a clarion call against what they saw to be a serious threat to—well, to what? Why had the rather peaceful plain of Bible translations—to each his own, there's room enough for all—tilted into a sheer cliff down which one would tumble into heresy if one surrendered one's position at the peak?

Several realities warrant recognition here—realities that some of the zealots have failed to see clearly enough.[3] First, all translations have infelicities, and even outright errors. Despite our best intentions, even in committees (and sometimes especially in committees), we human beings make mistakes. No translation is perfect.

Second, in the very nature of the case, translation is always approximate because no two languages can be converted exactly into each other. "The exact word" isn't ever quite *le mot juste*. Something is indeed usually lost in translation.

Third, and perhaps most important, translation of gender language is especially difficult nowadays because English usage is itself changing, and not changing everywhere at the same time in the same way. Some of us still use *mankind*, while others have long switched to *humankind*. Some of us still use *he* generically; others scrupulously say *he or she*, while still others conscientiously switch back and forth between *he* and *she*. So the translator has unavoidable trouble trying to connect the fixed languages of biblical Hebrew and Greek with the moving target of contemporary English—one might even say, of contemporary English*es*.

Fourth, and perhaps most radically, some of us are making way too big a deal about relatively small changes. Yes, something good is lost when a translation moves away from the focus on the solitary godly person in Psalm 1 ("Blessed is the man who . . .") to the vaguer generalization ("Blessed are those who . . ."). That's why I memorized this psalm in the King James Version. But how much is lost, really?

Enough to warrant blasting a new version with a shotgun and mailing it back to the publisher? Enough to sanction financial threats to a Bible society if they don't cease producing the offending version? Enough to justify the dismissal of a seminary professor involved in the translation project a year before his retirement? Enough to keep a new translation out of the hands of people who would welcome it both for their own reading and for sharing the gospel with friends who might be very sensitive to gender questions? (All of these have happened during the course of this controversy.)

Conservative New Testament scholar D. A. Carson describes the disproportionate reaction of some critics as "Bible rage." One might well ask, then, since psychological and sociological categories beg to be employed here: What agenda could possibly be pressing people to such instant and insistent opposition?

Some critics openly articulate their fear that such inclusive translations represent the not-so-thin edge of a feminist wedge that will lead next to feminine language for God and from thence to outright goddess worship. To be sure, there have been some moderating noises from this anxious camp. Yes, they allow, some changes can legitimately be made in translation where the original languages clearly mean—in their literal words, not just their phrases—to include both men and women. But even these ameliorists allow relatively few. Making too many, it seems, might set off an avalanche of gender chaos.

Yet the record shows that not one mainstream translation has crossed the line from inclusive language for human beings to feminine language for God. Even the NRSV preface explicitly acknowledges that the one sort of change does not entail the other. Moreover, the inclusive language edition of the NIV (Today's New International Version, or TNIV) has been available now for almost twenty years with no discernible rise in goddess worship among former evangelicals seduced into it by inclusive language. Furthermore, since the Bible's original languages themselves contain obviously feminine language about God, an extreme position on this matter ("let's stay in this ditch so we don't slide over into the other one") is just indefensible—as we will discuss further in a moment.

Clearly, no mainstream translation portrays God as a goddess. None try to "improve" on the Bible by conforming it to this or that ideology. The more-or-less level plain of legitimate translation alternatives has not in fact been turned into an all-or-nothing cliff face of "Christian" at the top versus "anti-Christian" at the bottom. We instead have been gifted with a range of translations by earnest Christian scholars who have aimed at the edification of the church and the evangelism of the world by offering the Bible in the most accurate and user-friendly style of which the translators are capable.

Frankly, when it seems evident that Jesus himself used an Aramaic paraphrase of the Old Testament; when conservative Christians of all stripes enthusiastically support missionary Bible translators all over the world whose versions—because rendered by a few people with relatively few linguistic tools at hand—are always much less accurate than the English translations we are privileged to enjoy; and when hundreds of thousands of conservative evangelicals have bought and used such informal and freewheeling paraphrases as the *Living Bible* and *The Message*—well, it's difficult to believe that all of this sound and fury truly centers on the question of the crystalline integrity of Bible translation.

So if it isn't really about translation, then North American Christians confront a hard question. Has the fervor in this latest battle for the Bible instead been aroused by the clash of social and political agendas? One might suspect that certain Bible-loving Christians, in fact, have succumbed to the temptation to co-opt the dignity of God's Word for something much less ultimate, much less certain, and much less glorious—namely, the explicitly antifeminist patriarchalism so important to these critics.

The next issue does, in fact, give many feminist Christians pause as well—namely, the question of inclusive language for God. We have discussed already why Yhwh, who is not in Godself male or female, nonetheless predominantly is spoken of in masculine terms in

Scripture. I am loath to suggest that we alter the way God chose to put things in Scripture, and when it seems obvious that there is a great deal of theological freight carried by the gendered ways God has chosen to reveal Godself, I much prefer a conservative translation philosophy. As for how we speak of God in private prayer, public worship, pastoral counseling, and so on—there, I think, we literally enjoy poetic license to simply do our best to articulate aspects of the multifaceted jewel of God's glory, a phenomenon that is always finally beyond our full comprehension and description.

18

Women and Theology

PERHAPS THIS BRIEF REFLECTION RAISES A cautionary note regarding the semantics of our theology, liturgy, and so on. Changing an element here often means an implicit change there, and that latter change might be one that we might not want to make. Yes, we need to affirm—and perhaps affirm more often than we do—that God is not male. We need to recognize that the biblical accounts need reinterpretation from points of view other than that of the traditional privileged male. But let us also appreciate the multidimensional images of the Bible that contain important truths in helpful, balanced combination—such as the language of "lord" and "lover." If we're going to go beyond biblical images as we attempt to theologize in contemporary, nonpatriarchal terms, we must make sure that our alternatives maintain the best elements of the biblical system and that they maintain their appropriate relations. This is always the challenge in any attempt to improve on the tradition of our elders (let alone on the revelation of God): it often emerges that they knew more than we might think, and we would do well not to dispense quickly with their wisdom.

With this cautionary note still in the air, so to speak, let us confront the fact that among conservative Christians today there is all too little imaginative and scholarly exploration of new ways, *feminist* ways, of reading the Bible and constructing theology.[1]

Feminism, like all advocacy, is centrally about absence and presence.

It is about recognizing that people who have been ignored and marginalized are in fact right here, and there, and everywhere. And if women are *not* everywhere, then feminism asks, "Where are they?"[2]

Roman Catholic theologian David Tracy has called feminist scholarship "the next intellectual revolution." Yet this revolution has touched conservative Protestantism hardly at all in the fields of biblical and theological studies. This phenomenon is odd, considering the burgeoning field of *historical* studies of American evangelical women—a major category of the more general rise of American evangelical history writing since 1980, led in particular by the efforts of the late and lamented Institute for the Study of American Evangelicals at Wheaton College. There is now a large supply of theses, dissertations, articles, and books on women in American evangelicalism, as there is on women in North American religion as a whole. But in biblical and theological scholarship, women seem largely absent—both as subjects and as scholars.

Again, on the questions of patriarchy versus egalitarianism in family and church, it is easy to point to Alvera Mickelsen, Gretchen Gaebelein Hull, Catherine Clark Kroeger, and other well-published biblical scholars.[3] Social scientists such as psychologist Mary Stewart Van Leeuwen and sociologist Elaine Storkey have contributed much to this discourse as well. But when it comes to looking at broader questions of biblical interpretation, and to the composition of fresh theological schemes, one still asks: Where are the women? And more particularly, where are distinctive feminist concerns among those women—let alone the men?

Orthodox Christianity has nothing prima facie to fear about a feminist approach to the Bible. Quite the contrary: in the very name of the orthodox championing of women as the equals of men in the eyes of the God who made humanity male and female, orthodox thought should be eager to seek out views shaped by women's concerns.

One brief example can point the way. Let us take a critical, but also appreciative, look at one of the best-known books of feminist exegesis, now thirty years old—namely, *Texts of Terror: Literary-Feminist*

Readings of Biblical Narratives by the estimable Phyllis Trible, a former president of the Society of Biblical Literature.[4]

Old Testament scholar Walter Brueggemann—a favorite exegete himself among many evangelical and Catholic scholars and preachers—endorses this book in the foreword, a book that originated as the Beecher Lectures on preaching at Yale. Brueggemann extols it for getting "the interpreter-expositor out of the way so that the unhindered text and the listening community can face each other." Brueggemann continues, "The method utilized here makes very little, if any, imposition on the text. . . . [T]here is no special pleading, no stacking of the cards, no shrillness, no insistence."[5]

On this point, alas, Brueggemann seems clearly wrong. Facing the first page of the first chapter, the reader encounters an extraordinary illustration: a sketch of a tombstone, with Hagar's name inscribed above an epitaph, "Egyptian slave woman." Below this is placed something that sounds biblical: "She was wounded for our transgressions; she was bruised for our iniquities." Before Trible has even begun her exposition of the Hagar story, however, it appears from the imposition of feminine pronouns on the male pronouns of the original passage in Isaiah 53 that the hermeneutical deck has been stacked by something other than "the unhindered text." It is one thing to juxtapose Hagar's story and a messianic prophecy of Isaiah; it is another to rewrite the latter text itself.

The book ends as it begins, as Trible composes a lament for Jephthah's daughter by rewriting on her behalf the lament of David over Saul and Jonathan (2 Sam 1:19-27). Such imaginative composition might well be a worthy poetic response to the story. But when the "interpreter-expositor" decides that the best way to conclude her Bible study is with a nonbiblical text intended to compensate for the Bible's offensive silence regarding Jephthah's daughter, we must agree that we do not have merely the text and the "listening community" facing each other anymore.

In between, furthermore, among her helpful insights Trible often seems to be looking for trouble. For instance, as she concludes her study of the unnamed concubine who is raped, murdered, and dismembered at the end of the book of Judges, Trible pronounces, "Truly, to speak for this woman is to interpret against the narrator, plot, other characters, and the biblical tradition because they have shown her neither compassion nor attention." She also praises the subsequent stories of Hannah and Ruth as showing "both the Almighty and the male establishment a more excellent way."[6] This suggestion that parts of the Bible should be read as corrections to other parts, and even that some parts could serve to provoke even God to reconsideration, will be nonsense for traditional Christians who understand God to be, in fact, the Author of the Bible behind and within all of the various human writers of its component parts. This sort of interpretative stance cannot assist such Christians very much toward an appropriate feminist interest in Scripture.

Yet what would feminist exposition look like that saw God truly as the ultimate Author of the Bible? Let's look at Trible's texts in this light. Trible thinks the Bible's refusal to name this woman dishonors her. But perhaps the anonymity is a device to underscore her insignificance in the eyes of the violent men in the narrative, rather than to imply that she is insignificant in the eyes of God—for how can a Christian believe such a woman could be insignificant to the Father of our Lord Jesus Christ, who notes the fall of each sparrow? Trible suggests that such horrors are described in Judges in order to buttress the rhetorical case for kingship under Saul or David—who each went on to commit atrocities of his own. But, again, a narrator who is inspired by the Narrator would be understood instead to confirm Trible's own point: that sin is vile and vigorous, and no mere political scheme will compensate for resistance to God's law. Such a lesson does not show even these putatively "terrible" parts of the Bible to be misogynistic, but quite the opposite.

Phyllis Trible, it should be remembered, is among the more conservative feminist scholars widely admired in the broader academic study of the Bible.[7] What comes across again and again in such scholarship is an absence: the absence of God as Author of Scripture.

Without the unifying force of a single Authorial voice holding it together, the Bible can indeed fall apart into a welter of apparent contradictions and scandals, ripe for deconstruction.

To affirm the presence of God's voice in Scripture, however, is automatic for evangelicals, conservative Catholics, and other traditional Christians. In this brief interaction with Trible from an evangelical point of view, therefore, I trust it is evident that traditional Christians can both benefit from the lead taken by scholars such as she, and also contribute exegetical insights of their own based on their different methodological and theological presuppositions. Trible's isn't the only feminist approach to the Bible, that is; orthodox Christians can and should develop their own.

At the same time, most evangelicals and Roman Catholics have not been so quick to affirm the presence of *women*. And so we might pause to consider another conspicuous absence in the discussion of women and the Bible, namely, the lack of impact more than two generations of feminist studies have made on most orthodox Christian theology.

In our churches, of course, and in popular writing and speaking, the contemporary feminist movement has garnered a great deal of attention. Congregations and denominations have split over the ordination of women, and whole organizations have been founded to campaign for one or another viewpoint on gender. But beyond the political question of which sex plays which roles in the church or in the family, feminist thinking seems yet unable to find a home in orthodox theology.

Even among those orthodox theologians who seem most open to contemporary currents in theology—process thought, liberationism, postliberalism, and so on—and who call for renewal or "revisioning" of orthodox theology, feminist analysis is scarcely evident. But if good fruit can be harvested from these other nonorthodox theological discourses, why not from feminist studies?[8]

Consider the female figure of Wisdom in the Bible. This intriguing subject should not be left to those seeking a Goddess to complement

the ("male") God of the Bible. What about the female imagery used
in the Bible to depict divine care for God's people? We have seen
above that this is an important, if relatively minor, motif in Scripture—
so how do "Bible-believing" Christians acknowledge it properly?
How would a feminist point of view help us consider any one of a
number of theological issues, such as the atonement, the work of the
Holy Spirit, the scope of salvation, and the nature of the world to
come? And surely feminist insights can help improve such key
Christian conversations as those regarding congregational life
(beyond leadership issues), liturgy, apologetics, and our use of money.
We *don't know* what feminist thought could give us because very few
orthodox Christians are investigating it, and those who do typically
must do so without the support of their faith communities, who are
generally suspicious of anything of this sort.

Orthodox Christians affirm that God is not sexual and is neither
male nor female—or, perhaps better, that God is imaged in *both* male
and female human beings together. We affirm that doctrine readily,
and then go ahead and depict God as male. Not *mostly* as male, the
way the Bible indeed does, but *always* as male. As a rule, it seems,
orthodox Christians *never* depict God as female, even metaphorically,
and rarely even as transcending the categories of male and female. But
the Bible does. Biblically minded Christians ought to welcome at least
the feminine imagery of the Bible—as bounded and accommodative
as it is by the patriarchy of every culture each book of it originally
addressed. We should do so in our prayers, liturgy, preaching, and
hymnody—and most of us have a long way to go in that regard.[9]

Many Christians, alas, follow the same pattern in our treatment of
each other. We are happy to affirm for the record that men are not
inherently superior to women, that male and female together are
created in the *imago dei*. But then we *act* as if males really are superior: superior as topics for Bible study, superior to lead in church
and home, even superior to represent all human beings (as in the
so-called generic language of "mankind").

Where are the women? More basically, where is the female, the feminine, the "not-male"—in the Bible, in our churches and families, and *in God*?

Yes, we must resist incipient Goddess worship. Yes, we must resist the loss of rich biblical truth encoded in masculine language for God in the Bible and in traditional theology. But our fear of those losses must not keep us in a masculinist extreme. We must encourage more women to undertake careers in theological scholarship. We must hear women's voices in our churches. We men must ask feminist questions along with our more "standard" lines of intellectual inter-rogation.[10] And we must pray God to forgive us our sexist sins, heal our blindness, motivate our hearts, and open our minds. If the women are absent in biblical and theological studies, we all are missing out on half the Story.[11]

Discarding the "New Machismo"

WOMEN CERTAINLY ARE NOT ABSENT in our churches. Indeed, they continue to make up more than half—sometimes much more than half—of almost all congregations, right across denominational lines. The problem of "getting men to church" in an era in which secondary benefits are few for men in churchgoing is recognized almost everywhere—beyond certain regions of North America in which regular attendance still can help increase one's business, aid one's community profile, and improve family dynamics. (I have in mind parts of the Midwest and Southern United States and small communities in the Canadian Atlantic and Prairie Provinces.)

The fundamental problem is the feminization of orthodox congregational life. (And I'll focus particularly on evangelical Protestantism here, since I have studied it the most.) Historians trace this trend at least as far back as the so-called Second Great Awakening in the mid-nineteenth century.[1] A gender-sensitive analysis notes a number of coincidental and reinforcing trends in this respect.

Hymns become more sentimental, more focused on the individual's relationship with Jesus, and simpler both musically and lyrically—nicely catering to the rise of domestic music making as middle-class women have time to learn and play the piano for family entertainment. The current satire of "Jesus is my boyfriend" worship songs points to roots that go back to such classic gospel songs as "In the Garden," which sounds more than a little like a chaste but ardent stroll with one's beloved. Doctrinally and scripturally rich lyrics that speak of strongly campaigning for righteousness in the company of the King recede, becoming quaint and even perhaps offensive. Who sings anything like "Onward, Christian Soldiers" or "Stand Up, Stand Up for Jesus" anymore? And what songs even *sound* like those anymore, instead of the soft pop that dominates the musical menu of contemporary worship?

Preaching also focuses more than ever on emotions, individual morality, and one's own relationship with God. Likewise, it calls for responses typically associated with femininity: mourning over failure to live up to high expectations; seeking forgiveness for one's short-comings; longing for the beloved; yielding to his will; agreeing with him even in the face of one's own contrary opinion; obeying his every command; trusting him even when he seems not to be acting in a loving way; and depending for one's happiness on his favor and for one's very life on his provision and protection. Where is the reveling in the gifts of life God has given us along the way, the "normal" human life, as Dietrich Bonhoeffer put it, of exercise and art and work and politics? Where is the call to heartily and happily give one's best to God, and to enjoy working on the worthiest of projects with God as a gifted and effective team?

The activities of the congregation skew sharply toward feminine modes of interaction and service: sewing or knitting or cooking for the poor; offering hospitality to visitors, strangers, and the needy; sharing struggles and needs in intimate conversation and then praying about them; corresponding regularly with missionaries; singing in the choir; caring for children in Sunday school and throughout the week in daycares or kids' clubs; visiting the lonely or confined; pub-lishing a church newsletter; and so on. Where is the "guy stuff" on behalf of others: fixing cars, repairing and remodeling houses, chopping firewood, landscaping, moving heavy furniture, coaching sports teams, and the like?

As journalist David Murrow puts it, "Church is sweet and senti-mental, nurturing and *nice*. . . . Judy likes the warm family atmosphere at her church. Every Sunday is like a big family reunion. But Greg hates it"—as most men are ambivalent, at best, about large gatherings focused on talk, and talk about other people, relationships, and the like. Murrow continues,

> Men fantasize about saving the world against impossible odds. Women fantasize about having a relationship with a wonderful man. So what does today's church emphasize? *Relationships*: a personal relationship with Jesus and healthy relationships with others. By focusing on relationships, the local church partners with women to fulfill their deepest longing. But few churches model men's values: risk and reward, accomplishment, heroic sacrifice, action, and adventure. Any man who tries to live out these values in a typical congregation will find himself in trouble with the church council in no time.[2]

One can hardly fault men for avoiding an organization in which there isn't much to do that they like and there is a lot to do that they don't. It only gets worse when their women seem to really like it and can't understand why their men don't—or, worse still, when women subtly (or obviously) indicate that the lack of male interest is somehow a spiritual deficiency.

Yes, men paradoxically still mostly run the show at the top: as clergy, board members, and major donors. Yet in order to keep the show going, they must cater, knowingly or not, to the norms of feminine spirituality, since the vast majority of members and volunteers are women. So we have in many churches a perfect storm of gender repellence: a women's club run by a male executive—and thus a society with something to alienate deeply both sexes.

Into this picture of inevitable congregational dysfunction and decline have burst champions of rugged masculinity determined to save the church from these trends and set it (back) on the path of health and power. Whether the fantasy-spinning encouragement of author John Eldredge, who wants men to be knights and women to be princesses (a sentiment echoed by his wife in their book on this theme), or the profane bullying of preacher Mark Driscoll, who bemoans the "pussification" of the church and urges men to be hairy-chested heroes and hyper-hetero heads of households (yes, the alliterative heavy breathing there is intentional), evangelical men have been given a model for responding to their discomfort in church.

Driscoll's extreme language is all over the Internet these days and doesn't need repeating here. Eldredge is milder, and puts it this way in these characteristic passages, with dichotomies typical of this outlook:

> In the heart of every man is a desperate desire for a battle to fight, an adventure to live, and a beauty to rescue. . . .
>
> Little girls do not invent games where large numbers of people die, where bloodshed is a prerequisite for having fun. . . .
>
> Which would you rather be said of you: "Harry? Sure I know him. He's a real sweet guy." Or, "Yes, I know about Harry. He's a dangerous man . . . in a really good way."[3]

Alas, this New Machismo is not only a throwback to the norms of an earlier decade rather than a paradigm fit for the twenty-first century, but it isn't even true to the 1950s, or any other decade of North American history. Women were not nearly as passive as they might appear on *Mad Men* or *Leave It to Beaver*. "The man might be the head, but I'm the neck that turns it" was the sly slogan of many savvy wives. And the middle-class women who did stay home and feel the frustrations of Betty Friedan's *Feminine Mystique* were envied by the many working-class women, whether married or single, who were working outside the home as well as tending the children, trying to make ends meet, and not worrying about niceties of gender roles.

To be sure, not all complementarians buy into this motif; indeed, the last few decades have seen the emergence of "soft complementarians." These are men who formally insist on certain prerogatives and responsibilities in the home or church by virtue of their sex, and who do in fact retard some of the advances of feminism (e.g., the equitable distribution of housework and openness to female leadership in society at large), but who wield their authority more kindly and gently, so to speak, than their macho counterparts and sexist forebears. Indeed, churchgoing men of this sort are guilty of less domestic violence than any other group, and their marriages are among the happier and more durable.[4]

A proper balance needs to be struck here, therefore, a balance that emerges from reflection on a common figure in social scientific graphs of male/female differences and similarities. Such graphs—whether of physical size, tolerance of pain, aptitude for engineering, or interest in early childhood education—typically show two bell curves rising and falling along the horizontal axis (one for M and the other for F) that overlap more or less in the middle. This sort of figure shows that there are many and important strong tendencies along gender lines while many, even most, human traits do not neatly divide into exclusive male and female cohorts. Most men are larger than most women, true, while some women are larger than some men. Women tend to have a higher tolerance for pain than do men, but some men are tougher in that respect than some women. More men than women seem attracted to mechanical pursuits, whether in a profession or a hobby, but some women do become engineers and some like to fix and race cars. More women than men are attracted to small children (just bring a baby into a room of both sexes and note the behavior manifest predictably along gender lines), but some men are strongly inclined to care for little ones and some women are not interested much in children at all.[5]

The feminization of the church, then, ironically leaves out some women even as it leaves out most men. Some women much prefer to build things than to craft things or talk about things. Some men, likewise, thrive on relationships, conversation, networking, encouraging, and hospitality. The way forward in church life, as I suggested in the previous section regarding home life, is not to fret over "man's work" or "woman's work," or "masculine modes of worship, fellowship and service versus feminine modes of worship, fellowship and service," but instead to note the wide range of *human* interests and concerns and ways of being Christian and then opening up the church to accommodate them and help them thrive.

A church with such a mentality will then offer opportunities to build houses for the needy, à la Habitat for Humanity, and won't advertise it as a "guy's" project but as simply a project to which anyone can contribute. Women won't be stigmatized for participating—nor will men who are gifted in other respects be shamed if they don't. Likewise, men will join women in visitation ministries or daycare work, if there are such men in the congregation, and again the church will avoid the linguistic signals that fence off daycare as "woman's work." Thus the church leadership teams will be open to men and women regardless of sex in order to attract and put to work those *human beings* who are gifted in those particular ways. Few there are in any group who have the ability to see the big picture, think strategically, devise comprehensive plans, motivate whole groups, and evaluate results fairly. No group can afford to do without the women in their midst who are equipped in this unusual way.

Furthermore, as feminist epistemology reminds us, women experience the world *as women* and men do so *as men*, and in many cases such experiences provide importantly different, and complementary, perspectives and abilities. A man *by virtue of being a man* will bring usefully different attitudes, expectations, and talents to working with the youth group than will a woman. A woman *by virtue of being a woman* will bring usefully different attitudes, expectations, and talents to the elder board than will a man. Likewise, of course, we ought to pay attention to the fruitful differences among the variety of ethnic, economic, occupational, artistic, and other qualities people have in our church that can expand our understanding and ways of doing things. The most ancient layers of the Bible tell the people of God to treat properly the widow, the orphan, and the stranger, as well as our parents. How much more should the people of God be eager to welcome the perspectives and gifts of all manner of people?

There isn't a nice division between "woman's work" and "man's work," between "feminine worship" and "masculine worship," or between "male forms of service" and "female forms of service." There is just *human* work, worship, service, and so on, and in a wide variety. If we embrace it all, validate it all, and promote it all, then all women and all men will readily enough find their places and happily get to it.

And if there truly is something to gender essentialism—as I think orthodox Christians who defend heterosexual marriage as the only legitimate form of marriage must believe there is—then it will emerge most naturally in a situation in which all healthy forms of human flourishing are available. Rather than us trying to specify in this particularly fraught moment in cultural history what is normatively feminine and normatively masculine, it would be better to simply promote all that is human, and let men and women participate as they feel God inclining them and equipping them to do so. Whatever is actually real in gender essences will then be free naturally to emerge.[6]

Why, Then, Do Women Not Lead?

IS THERE A PROBLEM HERE? Are women *not* leading?

Scholars and journalists have noted for some decades now the leveling-off of female leadership—well short of their representation in the relevant populations. Women outnumber men in terms of university graduates, for example, but relatively few women are numbered among those achieving the rank of CEO and other high officers in business, or among full professors even within the putative liberal academy.

Avivah Wittenberg-Cox, of the consultancy firm 20-First, reports on her firm's international study in the *Harvard Business Review*:

> Of the 1,164 executive committee members of America's Top 100 companies, the ratio is still 83% men to 17% women. And two thirds of these women are in staff or support positions (65%) such as HR, Communications or Legal. Only 35% are in line or operational roles—and there has been no significant change in these percentages over the last three years.
>
> Meanwhile, Europe's companies, while progressing on Board balance in some countries because of quotas (or the threat of them), are still struggling to balance their executive teams. Less than a third (29%) of European companies have at least two women on their Executive Committees. However, this is better than the 20% in 2011. None have a female CEO. Of the 1,025 executive committee members of Europe's Top 100 companies, the real story is the continued and

absolute (89%) dominance of men. Of the 11% that are women, the majority (58%) are in staff or support roles, a tiny bit better situation than that in the U.S., in which the number rises to 65% in subordinate roles.

Asian companies lag far behind their Western counterparts. The top Asian (including Australian) companies are still the preserve of men. The vast majority (89%) of companies have less than two women on their leadership team. Of the 1,099 members of Executive Committees, 96% are men. Of the 42 women who are sprinkled among them, two thirds of them are in staff roles.[1]

In politics, the situation seems to be somewhat better. There are increasing numbers of women in political office at all levels in Europe and North America, with Margaret Thatcher and Angela Merkel setting the pace over the last two generations. Women have been mayors of major cities, premiers or governors of major provinces and states, and cabinet secretaries at the highest level. Yet the representation of women in this literally representative occupation still lags well behind the proportion of women in the electorate. (For example, the US Congress is made up of only 20 percent women.)

What about leaders in churches? The Hartford Institute for Religious Research sums up the situation thus:

The Faith Communities Today 2010 national survey of a fully representative, multi-faith sample of 11,000 American congregations found that 12% of all congregations in the United States had a female as their senior or sole ordained leader. For Oldline Protestant congregations this jumps to 24%, and for Evangelical congregations it drops to 9%.

Several traditions, of course, do not ordain women (e.g., Roman Catholic) and in some traditions the leader of a congregation is a non-ordained, "volunteer" (e.g., Mormon). The congregations of such traditions are included among the FACT2010 congregations without a female as head or senior religious leader.

Wave 1 (1998) of the National Congregations Survey found that 10% of its overall sample had a female as head or senior religious leader; Wave 2 (2006) found 8%. The 2001 Pulpit and Pew survey of

American pastors found that 12% were female, this jumping to 20% for Oldline Protestant congregations and dropping to around 2% for Evangelical. A 2009 Barna survey reports that 10% of Protestant congregations are led by females, and the 2008 Mainline Protestant Clergy Voice Survey found that 20% of Oldline Protestant congregations were led by females.

None of these congregational surveys track the gender of ordained female clergy that might serve as associate or assistant pastors, and it must also be remembered that ordained female clergy can serve in roles other than as pastoral leader. Common wisdom is that one would find slightly higher percentages of female clergy in such roles.[2]

I doubt that any reader finds these statistics surprising. Yet more than half a century after the so-called gender revolution, why do these patterns persist?

Before we get to that question, however, we ought to ask a second version of the preliminary one about "Is there a problem?" This version asks bluntly, *Should* women lead?

After all, leadership isn't for everybody. Indeed, it is, by definition, only for a minority. So let's not immediately assume that for a woman not to lead is a bad thing. Furthermore, lots of capable people—even most capable people—don't want to be leaders. They want to do a particular job, not lead other people to do particular jobs. My wife, for example, thoroughly enjoys treating patients as a physiotherapist. For her to become a "leader" would mean leaving physiotherapy itself to enter an entirely different occupation: health care administration. I myself am a professor and I love it. For me to become a "leader" would be to leave teaching and writing almost entirely to become an academic administrator as dean or president.

Still, the underrepresentation of women in leadership deserves a long look to make sure that there are such good reasons—that is, reasons that are both adequate and benign—to explain the pattern. For we might find that barriers remain that prevent them from releasing their gifts as they want to and as they should.

FACTORS IN SECULAR OCCUPATIONS

Why, then, might women not lead in secular occupations? (We'll presently take a look at ecclesiastical jobs.)

Because they prefer other work. Too many businesses demand a culture of competition while women notably prefer businesses that emphasize cooperation. Indeed, 30 percent of new businesses in the United States have been started by women not least because they prefer a different ethos. Moreover, in one survey only 15 percent of highly qualified women singled out "a powerful position" as an important career goal; this goal ranked lowest in women's priorities, versus quite high for men.[3] Political scientists Jennifer Lawless and Richard Fox identify an "ambition gap," as they call it, between men and women: men are far more willing to run for office.[4] But is this the right term for the phenomenon? Do women simply lack ambition?

American historian Jill Lepore writes that

> across all levels of government, women have never held more than a quarter of elected offices, despite the efforts of organizations like Emily's List and the Susan B. Anthony List. . . . Between 2001 and 2011, the percentage of women interested in running for office actually dropped. One reason is that, in those Sarah-and-Hillary years, it became impossible to deny that female politicians face outrageously personal attacks little different from the sort of thing that was said in, oh, 1872. . . . This climate makes it all the more remarkable that a record-breaking hundred and eighty-four women ran for Congress in 2012. A record number, eight-nine, won.[5]

Yes, one might say that more women than men "lack ambition," but one might retort that women are sensible enough to prefer not subjecting themselves to the serial and serious indignities that are entailed in the quest for certain high-profile positions. Similarly, women don't lead . . .

Because they prefer other lifestyles. Many women feel that too much time is demanded of them by their jobs away from significant others. In particular, executive and sales positions often require heavy travel. Women also find there is too much stress involved in the prestige, power, and money that is not adequate compensation, in their scheme of values, for the cost to relationships, family life, and simply the nonwork sides of their personalities. Many women, like some men, refuse to accept a narrow definition of life success that entails leadership in a hypermale mode: maximum individual power, maximum individual prominence, maximum individual compensation, and so on.[6] Many women simply refuse to play this terrible game, and if that's the only way our society will allow someone to lead, then they won't lead. Thus observers have been tracking what over a decade ago Lisa Belkin, in *The New York Times*, called "The Opt-Out Revolution."[7]

Because they fear losing their femininity. Men can aim at success—because men have defined the terms of success and have done so in masculine terms. Ergo, men can affirm their masculinity as leaders without tension. Women, however, typically have to choose between being liked as a person and respected as a leader. In fact, a woman seeking to lead has to learn somehow to be both feminine *and* masculine, and in exactly the right proportion for the culture (corporate, regional, ethnic) she inhabits. The old gender double standard has not disappeared: "He's assertive, she's pushy; he's determined, she's stubborn; he doesn't tolerate bad work, she's bitchy." We have yet to arrive at either *two standards for leadership success*, relevant to typically masculine or feminine modes of leadership, or *one* that blends the best of both.

Because they care for their men, their parents, their children, or their friends. Successful women who show great promise for the executive suite nonetheless typically take the "off-ramp" in order to care for others. (Two to three times as many women cite this reason for leaving a job compared with men.) Then, alas, they find it hard to re-enter. "What have you been doing all this time?" "Oh, dear, things have changed a lot since your day." Too much success, furthermore, can rupture relationships with envious rivals, male or female, or those left behind and below—and particularly with male partners who cannot handle being attached to someone who enjoys a higher occupational status and earns more money.

Because they accept second-class status. "Nice girls don't ask"—for raises, promotions, even for participation on high-profile projects, according to Linda Babcock and Sara Laschever's widely cited study of the phenomenon.[8] Feminist psychologist Virginia Valian agrees: nice girls don't demand attention, and they certainly don't complain.[9] Indeed, they tend to make "molehills into mountains," fretting over perceived slights, reacting protectively to any criticism rather than learning from it and moving on, insisting on perfection before they can sign off on a project or propose a new one, overpreparing themselves for any challenge—and thus relegating themselves perpetually to the sidelines. "What doomed the women . . . was not their actual ability to do well. . . . They were as able as the men were. What held them back was the choice they made not to try."[10]

Because they haven't learned "man-culture." It is a fairly basic anthropological principle: since men have set the norms for leadership, women who fail to understand and participate in the culture of leadership established by men necessarily will fail in that culture. Men tend to bond over sports, both as spectators and as participants, especially the leisurely conversation that is the standard golf game. Women who "don't get it" will certainly not get it. I don't mean only that they will fail to understand the ubiquitous sports metaphors and references, although that is hardly a small matter in any social group: "in-language" serves to demarcate truly who is "in" and who is "out." But women who do not participate in these male bonding exercises also will certainly not be there when important friendships are formed, trust is established, signals of mutual affinity and support are shared—in sum, when all those crucial clues are displayed that, in a world of bewildering and dangerous alternatives, assure me that *this is a good guy. I can work with him.*

Feminists have traced differences in male and female cognition and discourse, and women tend, naturally enough, to prefer female styles. But if men are running the show, women will need to adapt to male preferences or face the predictable consequences. And, as we have already seen, when men have been able almost exclusively to provide the answers to the key question, "Who looks and sounds like a leader?" women will have to think hard about how they can insert themselves into that paradigm—or be marginalized by it.

Because women don't lead. It is much more difficult to do something if you haven't seen someone like you do it. It is not only more difficult to actually perform the task, it is more difficult even to attempt it. "Who am I to captain that ship, or wrestle that steer, or drive that dump truck, or sew that dress? I can't imagine doing that"—because I have never seen anyone remotely like me do it. Women suffer from a lack of both role models and mentors, authoritative figures who give permission, set examples, and render advice. As psychiatrist Anna Fels writes, women lack ambition partly because they lack an "imagined future." You have to be able to see vividly that to which you aspire in order to marshal the fortitude to persist in striving for it.[11]

And it is good news for women to recognize what they themselves are doing and not doing in regard to their not-leading. As African American leaders have recognized regarding racism and black initiative, to claim only to be a victim is to relinquish all agency and, frankly, all hope. This list shows that, according to female leaders and feminist scholars, there is much that women can do, or do differently, to help themselves and help each other take their rightful place among our leaders.

Having said that, however, it is hardly the case that women don't lead merely because they themselves make decisions that keep them from leading. Other factors need to be acknowledged as well.

Because other people resist them as leaders. Men do. Women do. Resistance to female pilots, female surgeons, female police officers, female professors, female judges, female business executives, and female pastors is still obvious and widespread. Furthermore, women are not offered opportunities to lead because of expectations held by both men and women that such opportunities will be wasted on

them—or, at least, will be not be fully exploited. Why spend a pre-
cious medical school spot on a woman who will likely work less than
a man when she does work, will take months or years away from the
profession to raise children, and will never aspire to the rigors of
specialization but will opt for family practice or, perhaps, that least-
admired of the specialties, pediatrics? And, statistically, not all of
these expectations are erroneous, as more women than men *do* leave
the professional fast track and *do* refuse to pay the price necessary for
the top executive jobs. Indeed, women don't get to be leaders even if
they do aspire to those top jobs . . .

Because organizations promote pathologically. Eighty-hour
workweeks aren't good for *anyone* or for any *organization*. "Leadership" is also construed badly at the highest levels. Think of corporate heroes such as Jack Welch of General Electric or Steve Jobs of
Apple, men with notoriously abusive personalities whose other talents
nonetheless helped their companies thrive. When are we going to
rethink these jobs to get the best people to take them, not just try to
find the best people who are willing to pay this kind of price for them?
Would the best emergency room nurse or physician necessarily be
drawn from the ranks of those willing to starve themselves of sleep?
Would the best pastor be drawn from the ranks of those willing to
neglect their families in order to perform more church work?

"People skills," a zone in which women tend to outperform men,
are routinely attached to middle, not upper, management. And
since women do tend much more than do men to take time away
from their careers to raise children (and there is that nagging biological reality of only one sex being able to bear those children),
clearly not enough effort is yet being made in business and the professions to find ways to keep good women employed well so that at
least some do get promoted to positions from which they can bless
everyone else in the organization.

Because men make it difficult—in all of the previous respects. If
men continue to hold most of the power in our society—and who
doubts that we do?—and if women are somehow being prevented

from something in our society, in this case leadership—and who doubts that they are?—then it follows that, whatever else we say about women's own attitudes, aspirations, and choices, the buck still stops at the big desk—behind which sits a man. My point here is that I don't actually have to prove that men are doing something to women— whether by statistics, history, or anecdotes. I can conclude that we are by sheer syllogistic logic.

One might call this a case of "blaming the victor." So be it. Things will change not just when women change, of course, but when we all change: when we together think and feel differently about sex and gender, and particularly about women in leadership, and when we raise new generations with different schemas, with both better prejudices and better convictions.

There is a weird phenomenon widely reported on now, however, among couples that feature anything like the Supermom who is trying to do it all. And it is a very different kind of "blaming the victor." Even those relatively few women who manage to juggle an interesting career with a full home life and a lasting relationship with a man sometimes find themselves resented by their men precisely because of their competence. The fragile male ego finds no place to call his own, no territory to claim as the zone of his superiority. (Meanwhile, "having a husband creates an extra seven hours a week of housework for women, according to a University of Michigan study of a nationally representative sample of U.S. families. For men, the picture is very different: A wife saves men from about an hour of housework a week."[12]) The central problem here, however, is that there is evidence that women hold themselves back (a stronger term would be "self-sabotage") in order not to threaten their partners' self-image. Couples in which the woman earns more than the man—or even seems likely to do so—are fraught with more problems, tend to have overworking women take on still more of the housework, and result more often in divorce. Somehow women sense this and many of them throttle down in their paid work to compensate.[13] We men have a lot to answer for.

FACTORS IN CHURCH LEADERSHIP

In the church, of course, many of these factors operate as well. But the church also adds distinctive friction to the ascent of women to leadership positions.

Because of terrible theology. Formerly, in the church as in the wider culture, women were seen as literally inferior to men. Dressed up with biblical phrasing, women were the "weaker vessel," by which was meant not what we saw Peter likely meant (physically smaller and economically, socially, and politically much more vulnerable), but irrational, intemperate, (merely) intuitive, and the like. They were obviously unsuitable for the rational, calm, and analytical requirements of command. The New Machismo, as we have seen, perpetuates such ideas as "men are givers, women are receivers" propagated by male pastors who seem fixated on sex and who thus draw from the physical equipment of sexual intercourse a pattern to govern all husband/wife and male/female interactions.

A feminist, however, might reply that such a view is too narrowly focused. We recall that during the act of reproduction, the man does contribute a sperm cell, but a woman contributes, equally, an ovum. Then, however, the woman's body contributes *everything else* to the development of that child. Once that child is born, moreover, her body *gives* the nourishment necessary to sustain that child, male or female, who is the very embodiment of needy receptivity. So much, then, for the man giving and the woman receiving (as we recall the apostle Paul reversing the relationship in 1 Cor 11:12).

One has to wonder, What use is this kind of theologizing, anyway? What outcome is in view? Are women *not* supposed to take initiative? To lead ever, in any way? And why is *taking initiative* synonymous with *leadership* anyhow, versus, for example, seeing leadership also in terms of the coordination of various initiatives to unite the group in a cooperative synthesis toward its goals? No: this is all just bad theology.

Because of the aura of divine authority. In the minds of far too many Christians, questioning traditional understandings of gender means questioning the Bible itself, since the Bible purportedly is nothing but simple and clear on this matter. Questioning tradition cannot be understood as merely an honest difference of interpretation of a complex matter (and, indeed, a complex source document), but has to be portrayed as a willful misconstrual of what is plain. And questioning the Bible, which is the very Word of God, thus means questioning God, which is apostasy. Down the slippery slope we slide: one moment we are wondering aloud about whether 1 Timothy 2 is quite so evidently clear as has been claimed; the next we are being excommunicated as wolves ravening God's sheep.

What we are doing here is not just taking or leaving the clear Word of God. We are engaging in theology, which is difficult and complex work among a wide range of challenging sources. This is *our* work, as fallible human beings, and thus it is always open to revision as God grants us more light and as we open ourselves up to it. In some instances, furthermore, the situation becomes even more complex as God ordains a practice for one group of Christians that he doesn't for others. Consider the differences set out in Acts 15 between Jewish and Gentile Christians, or the evolution of the wide range of church polities, or the diversity of styles of liturgy and music, and so on. Insisting, therefore, that there can ever and always be only one way to read every passage and draw every conclusion and formulate every application universally and timelessly is not only absurd but also is not in keeping with the way the people of God treat the Word of God in the pages of Scripture itself.

We must not, therefore, let some putative glory of divine authority dazzle us away from undertaking the hard, careful, and slow work of sorting through the relevant theological materials and constructing, with God's help, the best interpretation of his revelation to us that we can. We do not have to find the One Perfect Interpretation in every case. We instead are obliged to hear God speaking to us here and now, guiding us by the Holy Spirit in our particular set of challenges according to his written Word, with the help of the church's tradition and contemporary scholarship and the insights we have gained through experience. And we then faithfully obey the Word we have received, however partially and distortedly we may have understood it, all the while remaining open to more light on the subject from God.

Similarly, we must beware the resistance to any gender revision . . .

Because the stakes are too high: the very gospel itself. This, frankly, is a mistake commonly made on more than one side of this discussion. One will hear the charge that "the gospel is at stake" from those defending tradition, to be sure, but also from those advocating immediate and sweeping change from the egalitarian side.

Yet while the questions surrounding gender are undoubtedly important—which is why you and I have invested in this discussion!—they are not the heart of the gospel itself. That distinction is integral, in fact, to the interpretation I have offered in this book. Precisely because gender is a secondary issue, absolute purity on the issue could be compromised for the sake of an even greater good: the furtherance of the gospel. Were gender equality truly a matter of gospel first principles, then Jesus and Paul, as have seen, become unintelligible (at best), and missionaries today in patriarchal cultures must immediately stop accommodating themselves to local customs and risk death or deportation—as these faithful people surely would if the gospel itself truly were at stake. So let us refuse to let the rhetoric escalate to an indefensible level, let us calm down, and let us consider our actual options in this place and time before the Word of God.

Because men are there first. As we have seen in the culture at large, within the church as well men have defined the actual roles of leaders and the criteria by which all of us are to judge their success. Processes and principles of appointment and promotion have been constructed by men. According to our own theology, then, much less any sort of critical sociology, we can expect to find that the institutions led by men, including the leadership structures of those institutions, tend strongly to defend male interest and privilege. How could we expect otherwise?

Women have been helping each other forever. They certainly don't need a man to tell them how to deal with all of these challenges and solve all of these problems. But if a large part of the problem is with, indeed, men, then perhaps this man can conclude by offering some personal reflections on a key question. For if men don't want to change things, alas, things generally won't change.

How to Change a Mind

I BELIEVE IN RATIONAL ARGUMENT BASED on worthy evidence. Obviously, I believe in theological argument in particular, and have spent a fair bit of my time and yours in setting out an argument for general equality. But a change of mind on this question, as on so many others, is more than the transfer of rational allegiance from one concept to another. It *is* that, but it is more than that. It is, as most important conversions are, also a change of *heart*.[1]

Aristotle suggests that the speaker intent on persuasion must employ three modes of speech: *logos* (appeal to reason), *ethos* (appeal to a way of being), and *pathos* (appeal to the affections). From the male scholars I have read who defended egalitarianism, I received both *logos* (good arguments) and *ethos* (examples of how to be Christian, feminist, and male). From women—writers, speakers, and acquaintances—I received further *logos*, but I also needed to receive, and did receive, the crucial gift of *pathos*. I needed to *feel* something of the *pain* of patriarchy: of being interrupted or ignored in conversation, of being passed over for recognition and promotion, of receiving condescension or suspicion instead of welcome partnership. And I needed to be confronted with their anger, with their refusal to be treated this way anymore.

Women have entrusted me with great gifts: their *stories* and their *feelings* about what they have been through and continue to encounter. My wife has told me of how people frequently ignore her or interrupt her or even just walk into her on a street without apparently seeing her. Female friends, colleagues, and students have testified to the suffering they have endured—from conversational condescension to professional marginalization to marital oppression to actual sexual or physical abuse. We men will not change until we *want* to change, and one of the most powerful motives we will have for changing our minds is to alleviate the suffering of the women we admire and love— suffering that is obvious to women but often unseen by us men. I know it may seem incredible to women that men can be so obtuse, but people of color will testify that we white North Americans are similarly obtuse about racism. Poor people will testify that we wealthy people are obtuse about financial differences. And tradespeople will testify that we professionals are obtuse about class distinctions.

We men usually don't see how we dominate conversations, for instance. We figure that anyone who has something to say will just say it, so those silent women must not have anything to say—and, we sadly conclude, must not be all that bright or all that motivated. We don't see how our feelings for women can take interactions that are supposed to be constructive and mutually beneficial and divert them into sexual games that no one should have to play, and especially not in a work- or church-related context. We don't see how we unconsciously disregard women's abilities and interests, and *because* those decisions are unconscious, the women themselves will never know exactly what happened: they just somehow (again) won't get the opportunity, or the honor, or the reward they actually deserve.

We men need to hear from women about what it's like to be demeaned, disrespected, or dismissed. Yes, we can be told by other men to shape up, and that can help. Men certainly have responsibility here to speak up on behalf of their sisters, on behalf of justice, and on behalf of the greater good that accrues to everyone as women are treated properly. But we will respond more readily to exhortations from both sexes if we *feel* it, and feel how important it is. We need this powerful impetus to compel us to undergo the strain of actually changing our minds and hearts. Otherwise, we naturally will stay where we are, in the convenient and comfortable paradigms we have inherited.

Furthermore, I have needed these testimonies, not just when I was transiting from patriarchy to egalitarianism, but *continually*, to this very day. My wife has reminded me from time to time, "You're not as feminist as you think you are." I used to bristle when she would say that, for I had congratulated myself on having *had* my "conversion experience" to egalitarianism and I was now a fully enlightened man, totally emancipated from sexism, and (let's be honest) a truly admirable person. But I have come to see, at least a little more clearly over the years, just how deeply entrenched are the gender scripts that I have tended to follow all along. I have *not* arrived at entire sanctification and I do *not* dwell in the New Jerusalem. I continue to mistreat women despite my sincere intention not to do so, and I have concluded that *only women can help the situation* by notifying me that, yes, John, you're doing it again, or, no, John, you failed this time to do what was appropriate.

Let me be clear that to recommend that women undertake such action is not—horrors!—to blame women for my enduring sexism: "Since you aren't complaining enough, it's your fault I'm still mistreating you." It is instead to say that *if* women want men to change in this way, *then* this is one crucial thing women *can* do to help us do so. It is another form of agency, however wearily many women will have to engage in it, alas.

I recognize, of course, that not all men want to be so reminded. Many women do not have men in their lives who want to hear what they have to say. All sensible people, therefore, need to pick their battles and their moments. So women today will have to do what women have always done: press on, regardless, to make the best of their situation, to provide good examples to those women and men under their influence, to voice their concerns where and when they can, and to hope for something better, if only for their daughters and sons.

Still, feminist psychologist Virginia Valian urges women not just to wait for a brighter day, but to speak up now, and *particularly* about the small things that women tend just to swallow and endure. She points out that repeated small slights can constitute large-scale social *patterns* of repression—that mountains can, in fact, arise out of the accumulation of molehills.[2] So women can and must do something to keep the pattern from being reinforced again and again in the "minor" interactions of each day. To use the language of Thomas Kuhn's "paradigm shifts," add your anomalies to the paradigm to help collapse it, or it will remain your prison—and, indeed, the prison that disadvantages all of us.[3]

Yes, we are to patiently endure each other's shortcomings and not overreact to the social clumsiness of day-to-day life. And no one wants to be written off as a whiner, much less a shrew. But I, as a man, join with Dr. Valian to plead with women to speak up *more*, to acquaint us men *better* with what's going on and how it pains you. We just cannot know what it is like to be a woman without you telling us. I know it's discomfiting and I know it's unfair ("Why, after all we've been through, do we have to keep teaching you men such elementary things?"), but here's the sober and inescapable truth: if you keep letting patterns persist, then *they will persist*.

We men, of course, have our corresponding imperatives. We must help to create safe places and occasions in which we welcome women to say the hard things, the painful things, the confrontational things that tell the truth about how things really are. We need to brace ourselves for their words that will dislodge us from our comfortable seats of automatic privilege. And we must prepare ourselves to act on what we hear, not merely to let women vent, endure it with impassivity, and then congratulate ourselves on our magnanimity. For if we listen to women and then do not change, we victimize them twice. And we render ourselves doubly guilty (cf. Jas 1:22-25).

All of us need to see *and to feel* in order to change, and we men (and the women who heretofore haven't felt the need to change their minds about gender) need the help of you women who have these painful stories to tell. Only then will we men, in return, give you the help of our asymmetric social power that is so long overdue. Most of us men really do love you; we just don't know how to love you as well as we can and should! Again, I fully recognize that we, not you, are responsible to sort ourselves out. But may I ask you women to help us, please, become the egalitarian men we want to be.

Acknowledgments

An earlier book of mine, *Finally Feminist*, set out my basic argument. The book you have here is a revision and expansion of that one—sufficiently revised and expanded as to warrant publication as a new book with a new (and perhaps less off-putting!) title. The earliest forms of these reflections were delivered as the Visiting Christian Scholar Lectures at Taylor University in Indiana and the Hayward Lectures at Acadia Divinity College in Nova Scotia. I want to thank my hosts at the two institutions mentioned, and especially Daniel Bowell at Taylor and Craig Evans at Acadia. My editors of the earlier book at Baker Academic spurred me on to better work than I would have done on my own: thanks to Jim Kinney and Melinda Timmer in particular. The following friends graciously provided me with critical reading of some or all of the original manuscript: Allyson Jule, Jennie McLaurin, Cherith Fee Nordling, and Robert Yarbrough. I am grateful for the research assistance of Allison Kern, Jennie McLaurin, and Alex Saleh in the production of the current book. I thank Andy LePeau and InterVarsity Press for the privilege of working with them to send out an improved version of these ideas to a new audience. And Jim Hoover did me the kindness of reading this new manuscript, the revision of which was greatly improved by his sharp insights, sensitive ear, and gentle nudges.

I love all my siblings and their fine spouses, but the dedication reflects the simple fact that I know the marriage of sister Cindra and brother-in-law Daniel best and have had many occasions to both observe and be graciously served by their partnership in Christ.

My own partner, Kari, and our sons, Trevor, Joshua, and Devon, have challenged me continually over the years to a more consistent, sympathetic and humble outlook on questions of gender. For their tutelage and patience with a slow learner I am most grateful.

Notes

CHAPTER 1: WHOSE SIDE ARE YOU ON?

[1]Sarah Sumner puts it pointedly: "It's a debate between conservatives *and conservatives*. Those who are *not* conservative typically have never even heard of the conservative in-house terms of *complementarian* and *egalitarian*." "Forging a Middle Way Between Complementarians and Egalitarians," in *Women, Ministry and the Gospel: Exploring New Paradigms*, ed. Timothy Larsen and Mark Husbands (Downers Grove, IL: InterVarsity Press, 2007), p. 259.

[2]John G. Stackhouse, Jr., "Women in Public Ministry in Twentieth-Century Canadian and American Evangelicalism: Five Models," in *Evangelical Landscapes: Facing Critical Issues of the Day* (Grand Rapids: Baker Academic, 2002), pp. 121-39.

[3]This is not a recent development. In a book published in 1991, Elizabeth Fox-Genovese quotes a paper from one of her students at Emory University in which the student said that "feminism" to her meant "the denial of femininity and womanhood. It suggested lesbianism . . . , men-hating, and . . . aggressiveness." Fox-Genovese goes on to say that "to many women, feminism even betokens the destruction of family values and the defiance of divine and natural order." *Feminism Without Illusions: A Critique of Individualism* (Chapel Hill: University of North Carolina Press, 1991), p. 1.

[4]Sandra Schneiders speaks for many feminist readers of Scripture: "Whereas the Bible permits a fairly straightforward connection between the oppression of the poor and the stranger in the biblical story and analogous oppression of the poor and racial-ethnic minorities in contemporary society, the biblical text is not only frequently blind to the oppression of women in the Israelite and early Christian communities, but the text itself is pervasively androcentric and patriarchal, frequently sexist, and even misogynist." Sandra M. Schneiders, *The Revelatory Text: Interpreting the New Testament as Sacred Scripture* (San Francisco: Harper, 1991), pp. 181-82; quoted in William C.

Placher, *Narratives of a Vulnerable God: Christ, Theology, and Scripture* (Louisville, KY: Westminster John Knox, 1994), p. 111.

[5]It is apparent already that I am using the now-common distinction between "gender" (as the idea of what constitutes "masculine" and "feminine" in a given society or discourse) and "sex" (the biological distinction between "male" and "female"). To what extent, if any, gender and sex are actually, or "essentially," linked is a vexed theme of discussion in natural science, social science, philosophy, and theology.

[6]Jürgen Habermas writes helpfully in this regard: "Feminism is . . . directed against a dominant culture that interprets the relationship of the sexes in an asymmetrical manner that excludes equal rights. Gender-specific differences in life circumstances and experiences do not receive adequate consideration, either legally or informally. Women's cultural self-understanding is not given due recognition, any more than their contribution to the common culture; given the prevailing definitions, women's needs cannot even be adequately articulated. Thus the political struggle for recognition begins as a struggle about the interpretation of gender-specific achievements and interests. Insofar as it is successful, it changes the relationship between the sexes along with the collective identity of women, thereby directly affecting men's self-understanding as well. The scale of values of the society as a whole is up for discussion; the consequences of this problematization extend into core private areas and affect the established boundaries between the private and public spheres as well." "Struggles for Recognition in the Democratic Constitutional State," trans. Shierry Weber Nicholsen, in *Multiculturalism*, ed. Amy Gutmann (Princeton, NJ: Princeton University Press, 1994), p. 117.

Luce Irigaray further specifies in this vein that men tend to ignore vast reaches of reality in our typical speaking: "the masculine subject has . . . left behind him nature, woman, and even children." And when we do speak, men tend to offer our concepts and proposals as if they are packages we have put together on our own, and now hand on as objects to another, while women tend to pay more attention to the very "transaction" of communication and to those involved in it: Masculine speech "must convey a meaning in some way closed, in which the speaking subject converses above all with their own self and with speech. . . .

"The feminine subject, on the other hand, takes an interest in the relation between two, in communication between people. This subject is thus confronted with a new task as regards the unfolding of speech." Luce Irigaray, *The Way of Love* (London: Continuum, 2002), pp. 6, 24.

Some might retort that all this is simply a contemporary way of expressing the age-old recognition that women and men (tend to) speak and relate differently. Feminism, then, is marked by the affirmation, not merely of the differences, but of the equal value of the differences.

[7]I am aware of various typologies that feature successive "waves" of feminism and several competing views and agendas among feminists—for example: (1) a "unisex" view that sees men and women as interchangeable parts in society, so feminism means opening every place in society to women; (2) a "complementary" view that sees women and men as essentially different, but equally important, so feminism means altering the structures of society in order to profit from distinctly feminine differences; and (3) a "radical" view that sees women as superior to men, so feminism means the advocacy of lesbianism, women-only communities and other social structures, and the like. There do not seem to be, however, any detailed maps of this sort that have won anything approaching universal acceptance in this discourse. Yet I do not think that using one or more of these typologies will advance my purposes in the following discussion, so I need not advocate one or another herein.

For helpful introductions to the definition and history of feminism from a Christian viewpoint, see part I of Mary Stewart Van Leeuwen, ed., *After Eden: Facing the Challenge of Gender Reconciliation* (Grand Rapids: Eerdmans, 1993), pp. 19-113; and Elaine Storkey, *Origins of Difference: The Gender Debate Revisited* (Grand Rapids: Baker Academic, 2001).

[8]I also recognize, in this terminological morass, that some people resist the term *egalitarian* and similar terms of "equality" because of one or both of the following reservations. First, some worry that *equal* must mean "the same," thus ruling out any sense in which women and men are essentially different. I trust I have made clear that I am not supposing to have answered the age-old question as to whether, and how, women and men differ from each other. *Egalitarian* in this present discussion means "of equal worth, dignity, ability, and calling, and therefore not to be discriminated against on the basis of sex where sexual difference cannot be shown to be a relevant factor"—as it is in bearing children, to resort to the obvious example.

Second, some worry that *egalitarian* sounds like it is bound up with the assertion of "rights" in a kind of selfish crusade for the maximization of power for me and my kind. I respond that any leveling of *illegitimate* power and the raising up of the downtrodden is entirely biblical. So that is a good thing, right? To be sure, we human beings—that is to say, we sinners—tend to make trouble whenever we're in power, whether "we" are currently in charge or whether "we" will be in charge tomorrow. Revolutions never result in utopias. Still, justice is one of the Bible's constant themes, and the assertion of the rights of women is a cause that Christians have seen, and should today continue to see, as important. Indeed, the now-global conversation about human rights emerged out of the Christian West. It is the Christian understanding of personhood that grounds this conception—otherwise unknown around the world. So just because some Christians today are worried, and properly, that some other people seek to misuse the important principle of human rights for mischievous purposes, it should not cause us to relinquish this language and this cause. Yes, Christians—and everyone—are to be humble, self-giving and concerned above all for the glory of God, and not for our own rights. But let us not settle only for this one side of the tension in which God's people live and work. A key part of service to God and the world he loves is the just championing of the rights of all people and particularly of the oppressed. So say the prophets, the apostles and our Lord himself.

CHAPTER 2: HOW *NOT* TO DECIDE ABOUT GENDER

[1]Some good examples are the following: Robert K. Johnston, "The Role of Women in the Church and Home: An Evangelical Testcase in Hermeneutics," in *Scripture, Tradition, and Interpretation*, ed. W. Ward Gasque and William Sanford LaSor (Grand Rapids: Eerdmans, 1978), pp. 234-59—I register my debt to this remarkably fair-minded essay that affected my early thinking on this question; Ronald W. Pierce, Rebecca Merrill Groothuis, and Gordon D. Fee, eds., *Discovering Biblical Equality: Complementarity Without Hierarchy* (Downers Grove, IL: InterVarsity Press, 2004); Willard M. Swartley, *Slavery, Sabbath, War, and Women: Case Issues in Biblical Interpretation* (Scottdale, PA, and Waterloo, ON: Herald, 1983); Mary Stewart Van Leeuwen, ed., *After Eden: Facing the Challenge of Gender Reconciliation* (Grand Rapids: Eerdmans, 1993); and William J. Webb, *Slaves, Women and Homosexuals* (Downers Grove, IL: InterVarsity Press, 2001).

[2]Pamela Dickey Young, *Feminist Theology/Christian Theology: In Search of Method* (Minneapolis: Fortress, 1990), p. 17.

[3]For those readers wanting a little more help on theological method than I can offer in this slender volume, I offer my bigger book: *Need to Know: Vocation as the Heart of Christian Epistemology* (New York: Oxford University Press, 2014).

[4]I discuss this question of ethics in the "mixed field of the world" at length in *Making the Best of It: Following Christ in the Real World* (New York: Oxford University Press, 2008).

[5]For women in church history, see Lynda L. Coon, Katherine J. Haldane, and Elisabeth W. Sommer, eds., *That Gentle Strength: Historical Perspectives on Women in Christianity* (Charlottesville: University Press of Virginia, 1990); and Ruth A. Tucker and Walter Liefeld, *Daughters of the Church: Women and Ministry from New Testament Times to the Present* (Grand Rapids: Zondervan, 1987). For broader context still, see Denise Lardner Carmody, *Women and World Religions*, 2nd ed. (Englewood Cliffs, NJ: Prentice Hall, 1989).

CHAPTER 3: HOW I CHANGED MY MIND

[1]Thomas S. Kuhn, *The Structure of Scientific Revolutions*, 2nd ed. (Chicago: University of Chicago Press, 1970 [1962]).

[2]Jaroslav Pelikan, *The Emergence of the Catholic Tradition (100–600)*, vol. 1, *The Christian Tradition* (Chicago: University of Chicago Press, 1971), pp. 175-210.

[3]Again, readers interested in a rather large expansion of these epistemological musings are welcome to consult my *Need to Know: Vocation as the Heart of Christian Epistemology.*

[4]The Bayly brothers contend for such a "consistent" view of patriarchalism on their "BaylyBlog."

[5]"Even in simple subsistence societies there are almost no activities that are universally the domain of only women or men. The few exceptions center around childbearing and nursing activities, which are biologically restricted to women, and activities such as making war, acquiring raw materials and dealing with large animals, most of which require male strength. What is universal is the higher status of whatever is considered 'men's work.' If in one culture it is men who build houses and women who make baskets, then that culture will see house building as more important than basket weaving. In another culture, perhaps right next door, where women construct houses and men make baskets, basket-weaving will have higher social status than house-building. (This example comes from my own field

work in West Africa.) In fact, such differences may even become a basis for cultural chauvinism: 'they' cannot possibly be normal human beings like 'us,' because their men do women's work, and they let their women do men's work!" Mary Stewart Van Leeuwen, *Gender and Grace: Love, Work, and Parenting in a Changing World* (Downers Grove, IL: InterVarsity Press, 1990), pp. 113-14. Cf. Bernard T. Adeney, *Strange Virtues: Ethics in a Multicultural World* (Downers Grove, IL: InterVarsity Press, 1995), chap. 9, for a useful discussion also in international context.

[6]It must be acknowledged that the writings of eminent ancient theologians do contain some disparaging references to women of exactly this sort. (In brief compass, Elaine Storkey quotes Tertullian, Clement of Alexandria, Jerome, and Thomas Aquinas in *Origins of Difference: The Gender Debate Revisited* [Grand Rapids: Baker Academic, 2001], p. 98.)

[7]In fact, we encounter herein a deep irony, accentuated during the "cult of true womanhood" in the nineteenth century. Women simultaneously are told that they are not capable of leadership—by which is meant certain kinds of public leadership, such as business and politics—but also that they are extremely important in shaping the entire next generation, as in the saying that "the hand that rocks the cradle rules the world." One also might ask this question: If women are not capable of thinking straight, why put them in charge of teaching impressionable children, the audience least capable of detecting their errors and compensating for their shortcomings?

[8]Jonathan Edwards, hero of many evangelicals, including quite conservative ones, was perplexed on this very point himself: "Many women in Christian churches are much more capable than some of the men." He went on, "It will be found difficult to say what there is in nature that shows that a wise woman ought not to have as much power in the church as a male servant that hasn't a tenth part of the understanding." So Edwards reserved church leadership for men only, despite his obvious regard for women in general and for a number of particular women in his own life as spiritual heroes (not least his own wife, Sarah), because he thought the Bible told him to do so. Period. (For these citations see George M. Marsden, *Jonathan Edwards: A Life* [New Haven, CT: Yale University Press, 2003], p. 346. Marsden notes that Edwards did allow Sarah to exhort mixed adult audiences in the full flower of the Awakening, since she could testify to an extraordinary experience for the edification of all [p. 244].)

[9]This book is written partly in response to the dilemma that many contemporary Christians feel: God seems to have instituted patriarchy, but patriarchy itself seems unfair and unhelpful, particularly as it has given license to abuse through the centuries. I have in mind such well-meaning folk as Stephen Carter who, after remarking on the propensity of men to take advantage of their wives under the aegis of Christian "headship," then has to conclude: "God, for reasons no human will know, inspired Paul to appoint the husband as the head of the wife. But in our mortal fallibility, humans, mainly men, constructed a world in which the exercise of that office is often unjust. For that we should blame men, not God—not women, and certainly not feminism, which has been but the bearer of the tidings and has, in that way, played a role in the fulfillment of God's mysterious purpose." Stephen L. Carter, *Integrity* (New York: Basic Books, 1996), p. 151. I think we can reduce the mystery here and make much more sense of what Paul, and God, are doing in Scripture and in the church.

CHAPTER 4: TWO MORE THEOLOGICAL CLUES

[1]I discuss these matters of vocation at length in *Making the Best of It: Following Christ in the Real World* (New York: Oxford University Press, 2008).

CHAPTER 5: THE MODEL

[1]For indications of evangelical pluralism on these issues, when most commentators reduce the conversation to just two options, see Jack Buckley, "Paul, Women, and the Church: How Fifteen Modern Interpreters Understand Five Key Passages," *Eternity* 31 (December 1980): 30-35; and John G. Stackhouse, Jr., "Women in Public Ministry: Five Models in North American Evangelicalism," in *Evangelical Landscapes: Facing Critical Issues of the Day* (Grand Rapids: Baker Academic, 2002), pp. 121-39.

[2]The best book in the "redemptive movement hermeneutic" mode—that is, the idea that the Bible shows a steadily upward trend toward the full emancipation of the oppressed, and notably slaves and women—is still William J. Webb, *Slaves, Women and Homosexuals* (Downers Grove, IL: InterVarsity Press, 2001).

CHAPTER 6: EQUALITY

[1]Timothy Keller, "The First Christian," in *Encounters with Jesus: Unexpected Answers to Life's Biggest Questions* (New York: Dutton, 2013), pp. 81-102.

[2]See chapter seventeen for further discussion of this point.

[3]Among evangelicals of a previous generation, Paul Jewett's pronouncement came as a shock: "There is no satisfying way to harmonize the Pauline argument for female subordination with the larger Christian vision of which the great apostle to the Gentiles was himself the primary architect" (Paul K. Jewett, *Man as Male and Female: A Study of Sexual Relationships from a Theological Point of View* [Grand Rapids: Eerdmans, 1975], pp. 112-13). I hope that the model I present will be found to be in fact a satisfactory harmonization.

Perhaps it is worth making explicit that I have no patience with the common casting of Paul as the villain and Jesus as the hero in the drama of feminism in the New Testament. For one thing, Jesus and Paul have similar, not different, teachings and practices regarding gender, as I show in this chapter. For another, there *is* no "Jesus" in the New Testament except as mediated by other authors, since Jesus does not write any of the canon himself. So in the New Testament we have the Evangelists' versions of Jesus, yes, but we also have Paul's, Peter's, and others'—albeit in epistolary, rather than Gospel, form. There is no compelling reason to privilege Matthew's or Luke's version of Jesus above Peter's or Paul's. Finally, orthodox teaching about inspiration declares that Jesus is, in a fundamental respect, the Author of *all* of the New Testament, as it is the Spirit of God that superintends the production of Holy Scripture. So the pitting of Jesus against Paul both is a literary and theological mistake of the first order, and should be relegated to the dustbin of nineteenth-century German scholarship whence it arose. For more on this common hermeneutical mistake of privileging the Gospels over the rest of Scripture, please see my *Making the Best of It: Following Christ in the Real World* (New York: Oxford University Press, 2008), pp. 189-98.

Chapter 7: Gospel Priorities and Holy Pragmatism

[1]I trust it is clear that I do not mean *pragmatism* in the technical philosophical sense, but in the colloquial sense of "practicality," of "focusing on getting the job done."

[2]I do tackle the question of God's providence particularly in regard to the problem of evil in *Can God Be Trusted? Faith and the Challenge of Evil*, 2nd ed. (Downers Grove, IL: InterVarsity Press, 2009).

[3]This insight is typical of David Martin, who uses slightly different images to the same effect: "The lava of the Spirit runs along the lines of social fault; and the wind of the Spirit blows according to a chart of high and

low pressures." *Reflections on Sociology and Theology* (Oxford: Clarendon, 1997), p. 67.

[4]William J. Webb, *Slaves, Women and Homosexuals* (Downers Grove, IL: InterVarsity Press, 2001), p. 255.

[5]Julian of Norwich, *Revelations of Divine Love*, trans. Clifton Wolters (Harmondsworth, England: Penguin, 1966), p. 103 (chap. 27).

CHAPTER 8: ESCHATOLOGY

[1]John Howard Yoder says this: "The concern of the Apostle is . . . to assist everyone to remain 'free from anxieties' [1 Cor 7:32] in a world whose structures are impermanent, and not so important that we should concentrate our efforts upon changing our status with regard to them.

". . . Thus the Christian is called to view his social status from the perspective of maximizing his freedom. If an opportunity is given him to exercise more freedom, he shall do so because it is to freedom that we are called in Christ. But that freedom can already be realized within his present status by voluntarily accepting subordination, in view of the relative unimportance of such social distinctions when seen in the light of the coming fulfillment of God's purposes." *The Politics of Jesus* (Grand Rapids: Eerdmans, 1972), pp. 186-87.

[2]It should be noted that some translations and interpretations of this passage render Paul's advice to slaves quite differently: "If you can gain your freedom, do so." Such renderings seem less consistent with the thrust of the passage, which is socially conservative. But I also see no reason to argue strongly against this alternative rendering, particularly in terms of Paul's exhortations to Philemon that come very close to emancipation, which we shall discuss presently.

[3]Some missionaries, we should note, saw opportunities right away to campaign against social evils. One thinks of Mary Slessor rescuing twins in West Africa and Amy Carmichael rescuing orphans in India as heroic cases in point. But these instances seem to me to prove the general rule: One does what one can to resist social evils, but not at the cost of the gospel proclamation itself, and particularly not in a hopeless and ineffective crusade for social revolution—in which neither Slessor nor Carmichael participated. (Note that my adjectives are leaving open the possibility of a *hopeful* and *effective* crusade when circumstances permit it.) There are several biographies of Mary Slessor and works by and about Amy Carmichael in print. For the history of missions, see the standard, if now

somewhat outdated, works by Kenneth Scott Latourette, *A History of the Expansion of Christianity*, 7 vols. (New York: Harper & Brothers, 1937–1945); and Stephen Neill, *A History of Christian Missions* (London: Penguin Books, 1964). For a longer statement of the theology of culture out of which I am speaking, see my *Making the Best of It*.

CHAPTER 9: LIBERTY

[1]John Calvin offers some striking reflections on the theme of Christian liberty and obedience toward various scriptural patterns we have considered. I quote them at length because Calvin is not usually cited for his flexibility and pragmatism when it comes to ecclesiastical matters:

"Now it is the duty of Christian people to keep the ordinances that have been established . . . with a free conscience, indeed, without superstition, yet with a pious and ready inclination to obey. . . .

"What sort of freedom of conscience could there be in such excessive attentiveness and caution? Indeed, it will be very clear when we consider that these are no fixed and permanent sanctions by which we are bound, but outward rudiments for human weakness. Although not all of us need them, we all use them, for we are mutually bound, one to another, to nourish mutual love. This may be recognized in the examples set forth. . . . What? Does religion consist in a woman's shawl, so that it is unlawful for her to go out with a bare head? Is that decree of Paul's concerning silence so holy that it cannot be broken without great offense? . . . Not at all. For if a woman needs such haste to help a neighbor that she cannot stop to cover her head, she does not offend if she runs to her with head uncovered. And there is a place where it is no less proper for her to speak than elsewhere to remain silent. [Calvin, alas, does not specify that former place.] . . . Nevertheless, the established custom of the region, or humanity itself and the rule of modesty, dictate what is to be done or avoided in these matters. In them a man commits no crime if out of imprudence or forgetfulness he departs from them. . . . Similarly, the days themselves, the hours, the structure of the places of worship, what psalms are to be sung on what day, are matters of no importance. But it is convenient to have definite days and stated hours, and a place suitable to receive all, if there is any concern for the preservation of peace. For confusion in such details would become the seed of great contentions if every man were allowed, as he pleased, to change matters affecting public order!" *Institutes*, trans. Ford Lewis Battles (Philadelphia: Westminster, 1960), IV, x, 31.

[2]I. Howard Marshall concludes, "The motive of not doing things that cause stumbling blocks for evangelism is sufficiently widespread in the New Testament [as] to be taken for granted generally." "Women in Ministry: A Further Look at 1 Timothy 2," in *Women, Ministry and the Gospel: Exploring New Paradigms*, ed. Timothy Larsen and Mark Husbands (Downers Grove, IL: InterVarsity Press, 2007), p. 61.

CHAPTER 10: GIFT, CALLING, ORDER, AND EDIFICATION

[1]I recognize that some egalitarian commentators have suggested that this text does not represent Paul's own view, but is in fact a scribal gloss, or quotation of a theological enemy, or some other kind of non-Pauline interpolation. Chief among these contemporary commentators perhaps is my colleague Gordon Fee (*The First Epistle to the Corinthians* [Grand Rapids: Eerdmans, 1990], pp. 699-705). And the late F. F. Bruce, another biblical studies hero of mine, concurred with Fee (W. Ward Gasque and Laurel Gasque, "F. F. Bruce: A Mind for What Matters," *Christianity Today* 33 [April 7, 1989]: 24-25). Now, when Gordon Fee and F. F. Bruce speak on textual matters, we should listen—and I have listened. But I am not yet persuaded.

Even if I were so persuaded, however, it remains that dispensing with this text does not solve the several other challenges facing egalitarians in Paul's writings. I am grateful for this kind of excellent technical biblical scholarship, but I have come to conclude that only a *theological* take on these matters will avail. Resorting to finely argued revisionist technical scholarship—such as endless wranglings over the meaning of "head" in 1 Corinthians 11, or the interpretation of 1 Timothy 2 in the light strictly of local religious controversies regarding women teachers (e.g., Alan G. Padgett, *As Christ Submits to the Church* [Grand Rapids: Baker Academic, 2011], pp. 103-24 [regarding 1 Cor 11]; Richard Clark Kroeger and Catherine Clark Kroeger, *I Suffer Not a Woman: Rethinking 1 Timothy 2:11-15 in the Light of Ancient Evidence* [Grand Rapids: Baker Academic, 1998]; Linda L. Belleville, "Teaching and Usurping Authority: 1 Timothy 2:11-15," in *Discovering Biblical Equality: Complementarity Without Hierarchy*, ed. Ronald W. Pierce, Rebecca Merrill Groothuis, and Gordon D. Fee [Downers Grove, IL: InterVarsity Press, 2004], pp. 205-23)—seems to me to miss the patriarchal forest of the entire Bible for particular textual trees. Even if this or that text is shown to mean something other than what the church has understood it to mean for centuries, there is a whole lot more patriarchy remaining, and it seems to me a fool's errand—even if the fool is one with whose heart and basic convictions I stoutly agree—to attempt to purge the Bible, or even just the New Testament, text by text.

Furthermore, this marshaling of technical textual and historical scholarship raises for me the question of the providence of God. Why would God allow such confusion to continue in the church's reading of these passages for two thousand years, only to have it resolved in our own day— and then only by considerable scholarly heavy lifting?

It is possible that God so arranged things for the reasons I suggest, namely, to facilitate the church's accommodation of patriarchy until such a time as society was prepared to entertain egalitarianism. And at that time, in a wonderful coincidence, God then enlightened Bible scholars about the identity of this interpolated text, or that special context, and thus now facilitates egalitarianism instead.

I think it more likely, however, and a simpler explanation to conclude that these specially controverted texts are in fact consistent with Paul's teaching on gender—indeed, with the Bible's teaching in general. I have suggested, therefore, an alternative egalitarian treatment of these texts.

[2]I recognize that there has been considerable controversy in anthropological circles about whether or not there have been, or are today, cultures that can properly be called either matriarchal or egalitarian. I am not expert in this discourse, but my latest sounding of it indicates that the case for the existence of matriarchies is badly embattled, and the case even for egalitarian societies has not won the day. Especially since our own culture, however, has become officially egalitarian, there seems to be no reason to preclude the possibility that other societies might have espoused this ideal. It is grimly fascinating, to be sure, that so few have done so—if any have at all.

[3]Gordon Fee observes: "The well-known sociology of Macedonia corroborates this [pattern]. . . . Macedonia was well-known as an exception to the norm; from way back women held significant positions in public life. It is therefore not surprising that evidence of their leadership in the church turns up in Philippi." Gordon D. Fee, "Gender Issues: Reflections on the Perspective of the Apostle Paul," in *Christian Perspectives on Gender, Sexuality, and Community*, ed. Maxine Hancock (Vancouver, BC: Regent College Publishing, 2003), p. 75.

Having positively cited my friend Gordon Fee, I now must register an important disagreement we have on this question. He believes "'praying and prophesying' to be not exclusive of other forms of ministry but representative of ministry in general. And since 'prophets' precedes 'teachers' in the ranking in 1 Corinthians 12:28 and prophesying is grouped with teaching, revelation and knowledge in 1 Corinthians 14:6, one may legitimately assume that women and men together shared in all these expressions of Spirit gifting, including teaching, in the gathered assembly"; Gordon D. Fee, "Praying and Prophesying in the Assemblies," in *Discovering Biblical Equality: Complementarity Without Hierarchy*, ed. Ronald W. Pierce, Rebecca Merrill Groothuis, and Gordon D. Fee (Downers Grove, IL: InterVarsity Press, 2004), p. 149. I trust it is clear that I think one may *not* "legitimately assume" such a generalization. Instead, I maintain that Paul is in fact distinguishing among modes of speech that he sees as appropriate and inappropriate for women in church gatherings. Thus he provides a general rule—and also suggestive exceptions in various epistles.

[4]L. E. Maxwell, "The Weaker Sex," *Prairie Overcomer* 39 (April 1966): 130. Many others have argued this in our own day as well. For more instances, see my *Evangelical Landscapes: Facing Critical Issues of the Day* (Grand Rapids: Baker Academic, 2002), pp. 128-31.

[5]I pause to repeat that unless Christians reflexively take one of two extreme positions, namely, that "society is always wrong" or that "society is always right" (roughly congruent with the "Christ against culture" and "Christ of culture" models of H. Richard Niebuhr's classic typology in *Christ and Culture* [New York: Harper & Row, 1951]), then Christians are obliged always to keep assessing whether this or that dynamic of contemporary culture now requires this or that response—whether resistance, or affirmation, or something in between. "Going along with society" is not necessarily a bad thing, or necessarily a good thing: it all depends on just where society is going and how, as evaluated by gospel priorities. Again, for more on these themes, see my *Making the Best of It*.

[6]Indeed, I suggest that the modern drive for the liberation of women is a secularized form of biblical teaching about the equality of men and women. It is no coincidence that feminism emerges in a Jewish and Christian social context, among all of the other cultures of the world. And it is a matter of historical record that many of the early feminists were churchgoing Christians who articulated their cause precisely in biblical terms. There is now a considerable literature on this subject. Pioneering works in the field are Donald W. Dayton, *Discovering an Evangelical Heritage* (San Francisco:

Harper & Row, 1976), esp. chap. 8, "The Evangelical Roots of Feminism," pp. 85-98; and Nancy A. Hardesty, *Women Called to Witness: Evangelical Feminism in the Nineteenth Century* (Nashville: Abingdon, 1984). A good bibliography on more recent history and more general themes is Patricia Appelbaum, "A Bibliographic Guide to Contemporary Sources," *Women and Twentieth-Century Protestantism*, Spring 1999, published by Andover-Newton Theological School, Newton Centre, MA.

[7]William Webb points out something that is obvious to many in the pews, but is too rarely remarked in the literature: that the continuation of patriarchy by churches in this society puts a religious stumbling block in the way of those already converted. William J. Webb, *Slaves, Women and Homosexuals* (Downers Grove, IL: InterVarsity Press, 2001), p. 254.

[8]The chapter division between Col 3:25 and 4:1 gets my vote as one of the weirdest in the whole Bible.

[9]I recognize that not all abolitionists were orthodox Christians—or even Christians at all. But abolitionism in both Britain and America did feature Christians in the vanguard. And the broader cultural matrix in which slavery was raised as something to be discussed, not taken for granted, and then finally destroyed was produced by the defining religion of that society, Christianity—even as offshoots of and reactions to it (such as various forms of deism and liberalism) also contributed to the cause. For reflections on this point, see Rodney Stark, *For the Glory of God: How Monotheism Led to Reformation, Science, Witch-Hunts, and the End of Slavery* (Princeton, NJ: Princeton University Press, 2003), chap. 4.

[10]See E. Brooks Holifield, *Theology in America: Christian Thought from the Age of the Puritans to the Civil War* (New Haven, CT: Yale University Press, 2003); and especially Mark A. Noll, *America's God: From Jonathan Edwards to Abraham Lincoln* (New York: Oxford University Press, 2002).

[11]John Howard Yoder is among many scholars who note that "for a first-century husband to love (*agapan*) his wife, or for a first-century father to avoid angering his child, or for a first-century master to deal with his servant in the awareness that they are both slaves to a higher master, is to make a more concrete and more sweeping difference in the way that husband or father or master behaves than the other imperative of subordination would have made practically in the behavior of the wife or child or servant." *The Politics of Jesus* (Grand Rapids: Eerdmans, 1972), pp. 181-82.

I. Howard Marshall also asks us to take Paul's individuality seriously, as a particular man in a particular time and place, and connects gender with these other matters of social justice: "Paul should not be expected to step outside his time and see the consequences of his teaching any more than he is to be faulted for not commanding the abolition of slavery or the development of universal suffrage." "Mutual Love and Submission in Marriage," in *Discovering Biblical Equality*, p. 195.

[12]David Scholer provides this capsule description: "In the Mediterranean world of the first century the overwhelming perception about women was that they were inferior, that they ought to stay at home, that they ought to be submissive, that they ought to be silent, that they ought never to speak in public, and that they should have no role of leadership of any kind. Wives were to be subject to their husbands 'in everything.'

"In general, the ancient Greco-Roman Mediterranean society was structured basically as follows. The average age of a man at marriage was thirty, but the average age of a woman was eighteen or less at marriage. When a man married he was already a man of the world who knew how to live in society. He was a person who could function socially and economically. When a woman married she was still a girl who had never even been allowed to answer a knock at the front door of her home. A typical woman bore a child about every two years or thirty months through her childbearing years. She was always 'barefoot and pregnant' and at home. She bore a child as soon as the previous one was weaned. Although many of them died, that was her lot. Further, women generally had no education beyond the domestic arts." David M. Scholer, "Feminist Hermeneutics and Evangelical Biblical Interpretation," *Journal of the Evangelical Theological Society* 30 (December 1987): 416.

[13]This theme is at the heart of Alan G. Padgett's approach to gender roles: *As Christ Submits to the Church* (Grand Rapids: Baker Academic, 2011).

CHAPTER 11: THE PATTERN OF DOUBLENESS

[1]Iain W. Provan, "Why Bother with the Old Testament Regarding Gender and Sexuality?," in *Christian Perspectives on Gender, Sexuality, and Community*, ed. Maxine Hancock (Vancouver, BC: Regent College Publishing, 2003), p. 40.

[2]To this vast subject, a helpful introduction is provided in ibid., pp. 25-41.

[3]Some scholars suggest that Adam's naming of his wife as "Woman" in Genesis 2 parallels his naming of the animals earlier, and that he is to be understood as "in charge" of all that he names. The passage does not say, in fact, that his naming of the animals means that he is in charge: God put

human beings (male and female) in charge explicitly in the creation mandate of Genesis 1. But even if there is such hierarchical significance to assigning names, Genesis 2 is not unequivocally on the side of patriarchalists. Adam's recognition of the woman as "woman"—it is not said that he, in fact, "names" her—can be argued instead in egalitarian terms: that he sees her as "just like me" and simply uses the correct term for this phenomenon. That is what *ishshah* means vis-à-vis the term for the man himself, *ish*. Neither of these terms are in fact "names." Adam's "proper naming" of his wife as "Eve" does not take place, in fact, until after the fall, and may then be a sign of patriarchy emerging from the fall. Thus the "argument from naming" can be seen as supporting egalitarianism even as it has traditionally been seen as supporting patriarchy. I don't see either side obviously winning this case, and since the passage itself doesn't connect "naming" with either equality or hierarchy, I don't count the debate for much.

For a delightful change in rhetorical style from the way these issues are usually discussed, see Alvera Mickelsen, "Does Order of Creation, Redemption, and Climax Demand Female Supremacy? A Satire," appendix I to Gretchen Gaebelein Hull, *Equal to Serve: Women and Men in the Church and Home* (Old Tappan, NJ: Revell, 1987), pp. 245-50.

[4]Consider also that no major Christian body applies the strictures regarding widowhood that Paul outlines in the same epistle that complementarians invoke regarding the restriction of female leadership and public speaking: 1 Timothy 5:3-16. Egalitarians thus want to ask why 1 Timothy 2:11-15 is "timeless" and 1 Timothy 5:3-16 is so easily ignored. Is it really just because Paul invokes Genesis 2 in the former case but not in the latter? Egalitarians think that that's a lot of freight to be carried by a couple of ambiguous allusions. Another worthy attempt to set out what Paul is doing and why can be found in Alan G. Padgett, *As Christ Submits to the Church* (Grand Rapids: Baker Academic, 2011), pp. 89-100. Whether one agrees in whole or in part with Padgett, my point is made as one sees, again, how extraordinarily complicated even a nontechnical exegesis of this passage must be.

[5]Peter Davids puts things rather more sharply than I do, but he is well worth hearing on this point: "When addressing those without power (slaves and wives), [Peter] does not call for revolution but upholds the values of the culture insofar as they do not conflict with commitment to Christ. He then reframes their behavior by removing it from the realm of necessity and giving it a dignity, either that of identification with Christ or of identifi-

cation with the 'holy women' of Jewish antiquity. When speaking to the ones with power, however, he asks them not to use their power but to treat those they could dominate as their equals—for in fact they are. . . .

"The question for today is, Will men/husbands try to hold on to an authority over their wives that once was given them by the surrounding culture but now for the most part they no longer have? Or will they gladly drop power, as well as the pretense to power, and treat their wives as equals, reaping not only a more intimate marriage relationship but also divine pleasure?" Peter H. Davids, "A Silent Witness in Marriage: 1 Peter 3:1-7," in *Discovering Biblical Equality: Complementarity Without Hierarchy*, ed. Ronald W. Pierce, Rebecca Merrill Groothuis, and Gordon D. Fee (Downers Grove, IL: InterVarsity Press, 2004), p. 238.

CHAPTER 12: WHAT THEN?

[1]To be sure, male leadership only made sense if "leadership" was understood in typically masculine terms. Feminists rightly ask, What if empathy, intuition, relationality, subjectivity, and the like are valued as important ingredients of leadership as well? Then it would follow that even if men and women are stereotyped in this way, it would still be better to enjoy the benefits of women's qualities in leadership as complements to men's.
[2]See Elaine Storkey, *Origins of Difference: The Gender Debate Revisited* (Grand Rapids: Baker Academic, 2001); Mary Stewart Van Leeuwen, *Gender and Grace: Love, Work, and Parenting in a Changing World* (Downers Grove, IL: InterVarsity Press, 1990).
[3]And thus I repudiate even the "ultra-soft patriarchy" mentioned by William Webb and espoused by many others today. It is a "position" I find not only incoherent, but inchoate: I literally do not understand what such a position is, either theoretically or practically. Webb gives us little help in this regard: see William J. Webb, *Slaves, Women and Homosexuals* (Downers Grove, IL: InterVarsity Press, 2001), pp. 242-43.
[4]I. Howard Marshall, "Women in Ministry: A Further Look at 1 Timothy 2," in *Women, Ministry and the Gospel: Exploring New Paradigms*, ed. Timothy Larsen and Mark Husbands (Downers Grove, IL: InterVarsity Press, 2007), pp. 72-73.

CHAPTER 13: COUNTERARGUMENTS FROM THEOLOGY

[1]I suppose one might even conclude that two or more options are equally plausible, in which case one is free to select what one prefers—or, perhaps

better, suspend judgment until one emerges as superior. But I should like to think that on an issue of this importance and urgency, one will seek at least a preponderance of warrants on behalf of one particular option, and thus embrace it with a degree of confidence. Again, I discuss these questions in much more detail in *Need to Know: Vocation as the Heart of Christian Epistemology* (New York: Oxford University Press, 2014).

[2]Christian Classics Ethereal Library, accessed December 5, 2013, www.ccel .org/creeds/athanasian.creed.html.

[3]For those readers interested in technical theology, yes, I am thus implying my agreement with the Western church in the matter of the *filioque* clause of the Creed. But in this particular instance, I don't see how an Eastern reading would change things. In particular, celebrating *perichorēsis* (the "dance" of the three members of the Trinity as it appears particularly in the Cappadocians) simply begs the question of hierarchy: kings can dance with members of the royal family without anyone forgetting who is who. And we might note also that the Christian churches of the East clearly have no trouble endorsing sacred hierarchies almost everywhere one looks.

[4]Capitalizing on feminine grammatical forms and feminine stereotypes of the Holy Spirit to characterize the Spirit in female terms—as even some evangelical Christians have been tempted to do—hardly helps the feminist cause. To do so still puts the female in the minority position (two "males" to one "female" in the Godhead) and, indeed, the subservient one.

[5]Larry Hurtado, *Lord Jesus Christ: Devotion to Jesus in Earliest Christianity* (Grand Rapids: Eerdmans, 2003).

[6]C. S. Lewis is among the many authors who celebrate this hierarchy, albeit with his customary alertness to the limitation of all symbols; see his "Priestesses in the Church?," in *God in the Dock: Essays on Theology and Ethics*, ed. Walter Hooper (Grand Rapids: Eerdmans, 1970), pp. 234-39. Lewis is now notorious for his gendered language about a variety of theological points, including major ones. For example, in *The Problem of Pain*, he suggests that "we are only creatures: our *rôle* must always be that of patient to agent, female to male, mirror to light, echo to voice. Our highest activity must be response, not initiative." In this popular work he also commends Christianity in language that is almost impossible for a Christian feminist to stomach: Christianity itself, he says, has "the master touch—the rough, male taste of reality, not made by us, or, indeed, for us, but hitting us in the face" (New York: Collier Books, 1962), pp. 51, 25.

It is not my purpose here to "rescue" Lewis, hero of mine that he is. But it is fascinating to read a much later work on the same subject, namely, the problem of evil, in which he offers quite different-sounding reflections following his happy marriage to Joy Davidman and his devastation at her death: "There is, hidden or flaunted, a sword between the sexes till an entire marriage reconciles them. It is arrogance in us to call frankness, fairness and chivalry 'masculine' when we see them in a woman; it is arrogance in them, to describe a man's sensitiveness or tact or tenderness as 'feminine.' But also what poor warped fragments of humanity most mere men and mere women must be to make the implications of that arrogance plausible. Marriage heals this. Jointly the two become fully human. 'In the image of God created He *them.*' Thus, by a paradox, this carnival of sexuality leads us out beyond our sexes." *A Grief Observed* (New York: Bantam Books, 1961), pp. 57-58.

[7]A commonly quoted phrase from Johannes Kepler.

[8]I confess I find positively weird the attempt by Henri Blocher, whom I both like and respect, to invert this kind of argument to suggest that patriarchy was ordained by God *in order to symbolize* his relationship with his people: "Women, Ministry and the Gospel: Hints for a New Paradigm," in *Women, Ministry and the Gospel: Exploring New Paradigms*, ed. Timothy Larsen and Mark Husbands (Downers Grove, IL: InterVarsity Press, 2007), pp. 239-49. This would make patriarchy—a source of much misery for both women and men—a very, very costly and deeply problematic object lesson. Better, I think, to conceive of God making the best use he can of the cultural materials available to him—even as he commands the amelioration of those structures.

[9]It is perhaps not surprising that C. S. Lewis argues this way, given his Catholic leanings (see "Priestesses in the Church?"). It is more surprising to see it argued by that latter-day Puritan (and I use this term as both an objective description and what he would regard as a compliment) J. I. Packer: see his "Let's Stop Making Women Presbyters," *Christianity Today* 35 (February 11, 1991): 18-21.

[10]For a useful summary of these issues from a Christian perspective, see Elaine Storkey, *Origins of Difference: The Gender Debate Revisited* (Grand Rapids: Baker Academic, 2001). See also Craig M. Gay, "'Gender' and the Idea of the Social Construction of Reality," in *Christian Perspectives on Gender, Sexuality, and Community*, ed. Maxine Hancock (Vancouver, BC: Regent College Publishing, 2003), pp. 167-80.

[11]I argue this point at length in "A Double Copernican Revolution: Leadership and Membership in the Church," in John G. Stackhouse, Jr., *Evangelical Landscapes: Facing Critical Issues of the Day* (Grand Rapids: Baker Academic, 2002), pp. 37-45. See also the conclusions in Stanley J. Grenz with Denise Muir Kjesbo, *Women in the Church: A Biblical Theology of Women in Ministry* (Downers Grove, IL: InterVarsity Press, 1995).

[12]David Basinger submits this line of thinking to searching philosophical critique in "Gender Roles, Scripture, and Science: Some Clarifications," *Christian Scholar's Review* 17 (March 1988): 241-53.

CHAPTER 14: COUNTERARGUMENTS FROM CHURCH HISTORY

[1]See appendix B in William J. Webb, *Slaves, Women and Homosexuals: Exploring the Hermeneutics of Cultural Analysis* (Downers Grove, IL: InterVarsity Press, 2001), pp. 263-68, for a shockingly wide sample from the history of the church. And see Webb's appendix C (pp. 269-73) for a brief survey of social scientific studies of whether women are, in fact, more prone to deception than men. (Conclusion: they aren't.)

[2]Walter R. Martin, *The Kingdom of the Cults* (Grand Rapids: Zondervan, 1966), p. 225. More than one person has observed that Genesis 3 actually gives the intellectual nod to Eve, who at least seemed to consider the question of eating the forbidden fruit, while Adam simply took what his wife gave him and ate it.

[3]Patricia Hampl makes an intriguing point: "What is often overlooked, especially in recent times, about the Catholic tradition: in spite of its glaring refusals and inequities regarding women, it remains the only Western tradition that has an unbroken history of providing a respected way of life for women outside the domestic role of wife-and-mother. The work of a nun and of a monk is identical: the *Opus Dei*, the work of God—to pray. Specifically, to pray without ceasing." "Edith Stein," in *Martyrs: Contemporary Writers on Modern Lives of Faith*, ed. Susan Bergman (Maryknoll, NY: Orbis, 1996), p. 206.

[4]Janette Hassey, *No Time for Silence: Evangelical Women in Public Ministry Around the Turn of the Century* (Grand Rapids: Zondervan, 1986); see also Betty A. DeBerg, *Ungodly Women: Gender and the First Wave of American Fundamentalism* (Minneapolis: Fortress, 1990).

[5]R. Pierce Beaver, *American Protestant Women in World Mission: History of the First Feminist Movement in North America*, rev. ed. (Grand Rapids: Eerdmans, 1980 [1968]). Indeed, it is the missionary and "parachurch" (or,

as I prefer to call them, "paracongregational") ministries among Protestants that have opened up alternative paths to female spiritual leadership that the Protestant Reformation closed off by its repudiation of monasticism. Vast reaches of ministry—in leadership, scholarship, administration, philanthropy, and so on—were previously open to women as nuns as well as to men as monks or friars.

[6]A helpful brief survey is provided by Timothy Larsen, "Women in Public Ministry: A Historic Evangelical Distinctive," in *Women, Ministry and the Gospel: Exploring New Paradigms*, ed. Timothy Larsen and Mark Husbands (Downers Grove, IL: InterVarsity Press, 2007), pp. 213-35.

[7]A popular presentation of this contention can be found in Mary A. Kassian, *The Feminist Gospel: The Movement to Unite Feminism with the Church* (Wheaton, IL: Crossway, 1992). For important perspective on the fear of feminism among conservative evangelicals, see DeBerg, *Ungodly Women*; Sally K. Gallagher, *Evangelical Identity and Gendered Family Life* (New Brunswick, NJ: Rutgers University Press, 2003); and Julie Ingersoll, *Evangelical Christian Women: War Stories in the Gender Battles* (New York: New York University Press, 2003).

[8]Of course, no one does argue that—partly because Christian feminism in several quarters fell on hard times in the first half of the twentieth century, and partly because any sort of traditional Christianity was invisible in the social and mental worlds of the secular feminists of the 1950s and beyond.

[9]Bonhoeffer elaborates on this theme in his *Ethics*: "There are not two realities, but only one reality, and that is the reality of God, which has become manifest in Christ in the reality of the world. . . . The world is not divided between Christ and the devil, but, whether it recognizes it or not, it is solely and entirely the world of Christ. . . . Any static delimitation of a region which belongs to the devil and a region which belongs to Christ is a denial of the reality of God's having reconciled the whole world with Himself in Christ." Dietrich Bonhoeffer, *Ethics*, trans. Neville Horton Smith (New York: Simon & Schuster/Touchstone, 1995 [1955]), pp. 195, 201-2.

[10]Richard J. Mouw, *He Shines in All That's Fair: Culture and Common Grace* (Grand Rapids: Eerdmans, 2001). I elaborate on these themes in *Making the Best of It: Following Christ in the Real World* (New York: Oxford University Press, 2008).

[11]Stephen L. Carter, *Integrity* (New York: Basic Books, 1996), p. 151.

CHAPTER 15: COUNTERARGUMENTS FROM CONTEMPORARY EXPERIENCE AND PRACTICE

[1]Robert Benne and Gerald McDermott, "Thirteen Bad Arguments for Same-Sex Marriage," *Christianity Today* 48 (September 2004): 51.

[2]My sense is that this emphasis on doubleness avoids better what William Webb himself wants to avoid in his redemptive movement hermeneutic—namely, that arguments for legitimizing egalitarianism are then deployed for the legitimization of homosexuality and other "paraphilias." If (as Webb and many other biblical feminists argue) there is a kind of "upward slope" to biblical ethics, then what other subjects can be included in this scheme? What else that was previously proscribed can be revolutionized as *ultimately* just fine after all? Both abolitionism and egalitarianism can point to these *double* passages, the second type of which explicitly advocates the full equality of slaves and women. Such alternative passages are exactly what is missing in the debate over sexual diversity: *no* passage *anywhere* says that sex outside of (normative heterosexual monogamous) marriage is legitimate.

[3]To be sure, polygamy appears in the Old Testament as a feature of ancient Near Eastern cultures shared by the patriarchs and later in Israel as a nation. But it is nowhere condoned, and there is, I think significantly, not a single happy polygamous family depicted anywhere in the Bible. Quite the contrary: polygamy is depicted invariably as bad, and bad for everyone involved.

[4]Whether Christians should urge secular, pluralistic states to recognize or resist civil same-sex marriage is more a question of political strategy. And I believe Christians properly can disagree with each other in good conscience as to whether the gospel will be furthered more by one strategy or another. There are gains and losses either way: a Christian view of marriage might prevail in a campaign for traditional marriage, but in such a controversy Christians may also come to be seen increasingly as both generally imperialistic and particularly homophobic. Thus even some moderate people will become hardened against our gospel proclamation. Again, I discuss principles guiding Christian reflection on such matters in part 3 of *Making the Best of It.*

[5]A helpful survey of research is offered in Elaine Storkey, *Origins of Difference: The Gender Debate Revisited* (Grand Rapids: Baker Academic, 2001), pp. 76-86. Mary Stewart Van Leeuwen provides an extended dis-

cussion of the question of male/female similarities and differences in *Gender and Grace: Love, Work and Parenting in a Changing World* (Downers Grove, IL: InterVarsity Press, 1990). I have read James V. Brownson's argument that gender essentialism is not, in fact, crucial to this question, but I am not convinced: *Bible, Gender, Sexuality: Reframing the Church's Debate on Same-Sex Relationships* (Grand Rapids: Eerdmans, 2013).

[6]I recognize that in many instances deviant sexual desires might not be cured in this life, just as other psychospiritual pathologies might not be (such as personality disorders, which, not incidentally, mark many prominent clergy and theologians, among others). On some of the larger questions here, see Thomas Schmidt, *Straight and Narrow: Compassion and Clarity in the Homosexuality Debate* (Downers Grove, IL: InterVarsity Press, 1995); and Stanley J. Grenz, *Welcoming but Not Affirming: An Evangelical Response to Homosexuality* (Philadelphia: Westminster John Knox, 1998). On the biblical grounds for traditional sexual morality, see Robert A. J. Gagnon, *The Bible and Homosexual Practice: Texts and Hermeneutics* (Nashville: Abingdon, 2001).

[7]I want to acknowledge that in this deeply troubled world, some people will find the first serious and genuine love of their lives in a caring, adult homosexual relationship. Friends, including former students, whom I love and respect have testified to me of this pattern in their lives. I believe therefore that such relationships can be condoned, cautiously and temporarily, for pastoral, therapeutic reasons as accommodations to some people's particular injuries and needs. The church nonetheless is not doing such people a favor by "blessing" such unions, let alone normalizing them, but helps us all by upholding scriptural sexual and relational ethics as the ideal toward which we all strive in our sexual brokenness (and who among us is free of that?). In the meanwhile, we should appreciate the sober truth that some people are having to take the long way home, and a caring homosexual relationship may be a necessary part of that journey. In the small space available here, then, I simply want to signal that I appreciate that this is clearly a deeply challenging area of pastoral ethics and requires the best theological, psychological, and spiritual wisdom we can find.

[8]See Webb for a sustained examination of the case of homosexuality alongside the questions of slavery and patriarchy. Certain readers will note that I haven't strayed into the questions regarding "trans" people

(transsexual, transgender, et al.). I have declined to do so because, frankly, the science is still vexed regarding what these terms even denote; we literally are not agreed about what we are talking about, even as activists of various sorts loudly proclaim that the matters at stake are obviously clear. Civil rights for all people *as people* ought to be protected, and we don't need to agree on what "trans" is to agree on that. What *else* society, and individuals, ought to do in regard to the various phenomena located under the "trans" rubric is, as I say, dependent on the ongoing conversation among physicians, physiologists, mental health professionals, trans people, psychologists, sociologists, social workers, parents, ethicists, and more. Even feminists, however, do not agree as to how to regard trans people and the issues surrounding just treatment of them: see Michelle Goldberg, "What Is a Woman? The Dispute Between Radical Feminism and Transgenderism," *The New Yorker*, August 4, 2014, pp. 24-28.

[9]Caitlin Flanagan, "How Serfdom Saved the Women's Movement," *The Atlantic* 293 (March 2004): 109-28.

[10]Sheryl Sandberg, *Lean In: Women, Work, and the Will to Lead* (New York: Knopf, 2013). Cf. Christina Hoff Sommers, "What 'Lean In' Misunderstands About Gender Differences," *The Atlantic*, March 19, 2013, www.theatlantic.com/sexes/archive/2013/03/what-lean-in-misunderstands-about-gender-differences/274138; Anne-Marie Slaughter, "Why Women Still Can't Have It All," *The Atlantic*, June 13, 2012, www.theatlantic.com/magazine/archive/2012/07/why-women-still-cant-have-it-all/309020.

[11]Jill Lepore, "The Last Amazon: Wonder Woman Returns," *The New Yorker*, September 22, 2014, p. 68.

[12]This latter development is one that North American Christians should be careful about condemning, not incidentally, since it has brought a measure of wealth to formerly impoverished regions elsewhere.

[13]See Storkey, *Origins of Difference*, and Van Leeuwen, *Gender and Grace*.

[14]I have said some more in my book on the problem of evil, *Can God Be Trusted? Faith and the Challenge of Evil* (New York: Oxford University Press, 1998); and in my theology of culture, *Making the Best of It: Following Christ in the Real World* (New York: Oxford University Press, 2008).

[15]Plantinga, quoting a line from the film *Grand Canyon* as the title of his book, *Not the Way It's Supposed to Be: A Breviary of Sin* (Grand Rapids: Eerdmans, 1995).

[16]Gretchen Gaebelein Hull, *Equal to Serve: Women and Men in the Church and Home* (Old Tappan, NJ: Revell, 1987), p. 241.

[17]The history of missions must not be whitewashed. It is replete with examples of tensions such as these that strain Christian fidelity to the point that some values are sacrificed—for better or for worse—for the sake of others. Philip Jenkins points to the seventeenth-century Jesuit Robert De Nobili, a hero of Roman Catholic missions, who posed as a Hindu guru, adopted the local dress and—in what was clearly scandalous according to Christian ethics in general, but was done in order precisely to avoid scandal in that missionary situation—observed the caste system such that he refused to treat the poor on equal terms. Jenkins frankly acknowledges this contradiction of the teachings of Jesus, and yet concludes, "This represented a successful missionary strategy, and perhaps the only one that could have worked in the setting of the time." Philip Jenkins, *The Next Christendom: The Coming of Global Christianity* (New York: Oxford University Press, 2002), p. 30.

[18]I commend the concept of "hesitation" as articulated in Glenn Tinder's highly suggestive book, *The Political Meaning of Christianity* (Baton Rouge: Louisiana State University Press, 1989): "The prophetic stance is an ideal of taking full cognizance of our common worldly circumstances, being mindful of both our limitations and our responsibilities, and in that frame of mind waiting for God. We recognize the priority of waiting when we hesitate before acting. We thus take time to remember our finitude and sinfulness and to remind ourselves that the initiative does not belong to human beings. Hesitation is a formality required of us when we cross the frontier between waiting and action; it is also a formality that in the midst of action we occasionally pause and repeat. Like all significant formalities, it is a mark of respect—for God and the creatures with whom we share the earth. And it expresses humility: there are values and realities beyond our understanding and control" (p. 164).

CHAPTER 16: WHAT THEN?

[1]Nancy Nason-Clark, *The Battered Wife: How Christians Confront Family Violence* (Louisville, KY: Westminster John Knox, 1997); Catherine Clark Kroeger and Nancy Nason-Clark, *No Place for Abuse: Biblical and Practical Resources to Counteract Domestic Violence* (Downers Grove, IL: InterVarsity Press, 2001); Nancy Nason-Clark and Catherine Clark Kroeger, *Refuge from*

Abuse: Healing and Hope for Abused Christian Women (Downers Grove, IL: InterVarsity Press, 2004).

[2]For two very different reflections on this question—one personal and impressionistic, the other social scientific—see Nicholas Wolterstorff, "Between the Times," *The Reformed Journal* 40 (December 1990): 18-19; and Sally K. Gallagher, *Evangelical Identity and Gendered Family Life* (New Brunswick, NJ: Rutgers University Press, 2003). Both of these observers go beyond the question of individual prejudices and interests to remark on the social dimension. For some Christian groups, gender questions have become "boundary" and "identity" markers linked to even more fundamental matters of religious authority, theological method, and resistance to worldliness. As such, I would say that gender questions become almost impossibly large to submit to serious reexamination—and so they aren't.

CHAPTER 17: INCLUSIVE LANGUAGE

[1]For accounts of the resistance toward gender equality among American evangelicals at that time, see Julie Ingersoll, *Evangelical Christian Women: War Stories in the Gender Battles* (New York: New York University Press, 2003). For an account of evangelical mobilization on behalf of gender equality, see Pamela D. H. Cochran, *Evangelical Feminism: A History* (New York: New York University Press, 2005).

[2]Some material in what follows appeared originally in the following essays: "The Battle for the Inclusive Bible," *Christianity Today* 43 (November 15, 1999): 83-84; "Finding a Home for Eve," *Christianity Today* 43 (March 1, 1999): 60-61; and "God as Lord and Lover: Masculine Language Revisited," *The Christian Century* 109 (November 11, 1992): 1020-21. A pioneering work in this regard is Rosemary Radford Ruether, *Sexism and God-Talk: Toward a Feminist Theology* (Boston: Beacon, 1983).

[3]Among helpful guides to this debate are two books by evangelical scholars who cannot be faulted for a feminist bias, since they are self-declared "complementarians": Mark Strauss, *Distorting Scripture? The Challenge of Bible Translation and Gender Accuracy* (Downers Grove, IL: InterVarsity Press, 1998); and Donald Carson, *The Inclusive Language Debate: A Plea for Realism* (Grand Rapids: Baker Academic, 1998).

CHAPTER 18: WOMEN AND THEOLOGY

[1]Roman Catholics are trying to follow the direction of John Paul II to forge a feminism that is both traditional—patriarchal in some respects, espe-

cially in regard to clergy—and yet affirming of women as fully human beings. It remains to be seen how "feminist" this is, and how much it is just the Catholic version of Protestant "complementarianism." Still, it seems to be a more robust and extensive philosophical and theological program than is evident among Protestants. See Michele M. Schumacher, ed., *Women in Christ: Toward a New Feminism* (Grand Rapids: Eerdmans, 2004). Cf. Hans Küng, *Women in Christianity*, trans. John Bowden (New York: Continuum, 2001). More broadly, feminist theology can be sampled in these two fine anthologies: Ann Loades, ed., *Feminist Theology: A Reader* (Louisville, KY: Westminster John Knox, 1990); and Janet Martin Soskice and Diana Lipton, eds., *Feminism and Theology* (Oxford: Oxford University Press, 2003).

[2]On the following, especially regarding feminist biblical studies, see Cullen Murphy, *The Word According to Eve: Women and the Bible in Ancient Times and Our Own* (New York: Houghton Mifflin, 1998). Murphy's book, it must be acknowledged, ranges no further to the "right" than the scholarship of Fuller Theological Seminary, which is commonly seen to represent the leftward edge of North American evangelicalism.

[3]Along with the sources already cited, see Catherine Clark Kroeger and Mary J. Evans, eds., *The IVP Women's Bible Commentary* (Downers Grove, IL: InterVarsity Press, 2002).

[4]Phyllis Trible, *Texts of Terror: Literary-Feminist Readings of Biblical Narratives* (Philadelphia: Fortress, 1984).

[5]Walter Brueggemann, foreword to Trible, *Texts of Terror*, pp. ix-x.

[6]Trible, *Texts of Terror*, pp. 85-86.

[7]For a taste of things to Trible's left that covers many of the same stories, see Danna Nolan Fewell and David M. Gunn, *Gender, Power, and Promise: The Subject of the Bible's First Story* (Nashville: Abingdon, 1993). I thank Phil Long for this reference.

[8]Cherith Fee Nordling, among the few North American evangelical scholars to become familiar with a wide range of feminist theologies, notes that evangelical avoidance of feminist work is mirrored by typical feminist avoidance of non-feminist work: "Much feminist theology is poor—not because it is feminist, but because it fails to uphold a high standard of scholarship. Feminist theology is most often dualistically constructed from the perspective of 'us' and 'them'—the oppressed and the oppressors—and their methodology reflects this dualism. Women who write theological

treatises without consulting works by non-feminists (or men, period) . . . limit full-fledged engagement within the disciplines of theology and Biblical studies. . . . By creating a sub-discipline through reading and responding only to other feminists, these women fall into the same traps of the tradition they criticize. When theology is done only in the company of like minds and like interests, it perpetuates a narrow view maintained from a moral high ground. The humility, kindness, and openness necessary to learn from differently positioned texts and conversation partners seems absent from much feminist dialogue. And yet, if this is so, how will those who might benefit most from exposure to their perspective ever really gain access to [it]?" Correspondence with the author, 2004.

An unwitting witness to Fee Nordling's testimony is provided by a survey of feminist theology that is almost completely unaware of any evangelical scholarship on the question at all: Natalie K. Watson, *Feminist Theology* (Grand Rapids: Eerdmans, 2003). A superb example of feminist biblical scholarship from an evangelical Christian is Richard Bauckham, *Gospel Women: Studies of the Named Women in the Gospels* (Grand Rapids: Eerdmans, 2002).

[9]A thorough and fair-minded treatment of these issues is John W. Cooper, *Our Father in Heaven: Christian Faith and Inclusive Language for God* (Grand Rapids: Baker, 1998).

[10]Serene Jones provides a list of such questions in regard to the doctrine of the Trinity: "What views of women are embedded in this drama? How might a person whose character is shaped by the Trinity live as a woman in today's world? Would having the Trinity as the conceptual drama within which a woman lives make a difference in how she responds to gender roles? And, perhaps most important, does the landscape of the Trinity promote the full liberation of women and all persons? Is it a doctrine that situates the community within the drama of God's emancipatory will for creation?" *Feminist Theory and Christian Theology: Cartographies of Grace* (Minneapolis: Augsburg Fortress, 2000), p. 17; compare her list of questions on the doctrine of sin on p. 96. To be sure, some readers (I among them) would worry that some of these questions seem to imply that if the doctrine of the Trinity somehow does *not* advance the emancipation of women, it ought to be discarded—which is precisely the way more radical forms of feminist theology proceed. In this book, however, Jones appears to be centrally concerned with taking for granted the truth of the tradition

and seeing how feminist theory and classical doctrine can illuminate each other. So one might go back over Jones's list and tinker with the questions appropriately—but *some* such list is what feminist thinking can fruitfully add to the standard questions of theological consideration.

[11]Janet Martin Soskice provides an example of feminist theology seeking to use constructively, and not just deconstruct critically, traditional and biblical metaphors for God: see *The Kindness of God: Metaphor, Gender, and Religious Language* (Oxford: Oxford University Press, 2007). At a more introductory level, see Pamela Dickey Young, *Feminist Theology/Christian Theology: In Search of Method* (Minneapolis: Fortress, 1990).

CHAPTER 19: DISCARDING THE "NEW MACHISMO"

[1]Perhaps the best known of historical works in this field is Ann Douglas, *The Feminization of American Culture* (New York: Knopf, 1977). See also June Hadden Hobbs, *I Sing for I Cannot Be Silent: The Feminization of American Hymnody, 1870–1920* (Pittsburgh: University of Pittsburgh Press, 1997); several of the essays in Linda Woodhead, ed., *Reinventing Christianity: Nineteenth-Century Contexts* (Burlington, VT: Ashgate, 2001); Margaret Lamberts Bendroth and Virginia Lieson Brereton, eds., *Women and Twentieth-Century Protestantism* (Urbana: University of Illinois Press, 2002); and Patrick Pasture, Jan Art, and Thomas Buerman, eds., *Gender and Christianity in Modern Europe: Beyond the Feminization Thesis* (Leuven: Leuven University Press, 2012).

[2]David Murrow, *Why Men Hate Going to Church* (Nashville: Nelson, 2005), pp. 14, 15. This book has exasperating bits of the New Machismo—including citations of Leon Podles, who seems to think God is actually male—mixed in with a good deal of accurate and bold truth telling about its subject.

[3]John Eldredge, *Wild at Heart: Discovering the Secret of a Man's Soul* (Nashville: Nelson, 2001), pp. 9, 10, 16; cf. John and Stasi Eldredge, *Captivating: Unveiling the Mystery of a Woman's Soul* (Nashville: Nelson, 2005).

[4]W. Bradford Wilcox, *Soft Patriarchs, New Men: How Christianity Shapes Fathers and Husbands* (Chicago: University of Chicago Press, 2004).

[5]Evangelical psychologist Mary Stewart Van Leeuwen typically emphasizes the overlapping of the two curves to advocate for feminism against gender hierarchalists who make too much of the (relatively small) differences in most cases. I agree with her on that tactic, and I am emphasizing that typically large overlap for a complementary purpose here. I also point out, however, that the fact that there are two distinct curves ought to mean

something, and she never says (so far as I know) what that something might be. Indeed, as a defender of the Bible's refusal to sanction homosexuality, I am inclined to think sex/gender complementarity is likely both real and important, however difficult it has proven so far to specify. See Mary Stewart Van Leeuwen, "Opposite Sexes or Neighboring Sexes? What Do the Social Sciences Really Tell Us?," in *Women, Ministry and the Gospel: Exploring New Paradigms*, ed. Timothy Larsen and Mark Husbands (Downers Grove, IL: InterVarsity Press, 2007), pp. 171-99. Van Leeuwen includes such graphs as appendices to the chapter. For recent scholarship that points up stark gender differences exactly where one might not think to find them clearly differentiated, see Thomas Knecht and Emily Ecklund, "Gender Differences at Christian and Secular Colleges," *Christian Scholar's Review* 43 (Summer 2014): 313-41.

[6]I might say, with a friendly wink, that this is a kind of "performativity" not entirely in keeping with that articulated so provocatively in Judith Butler, *Gender Trouble: Feminism and the Subversion of Identity* (New York: Routledge, 1990).

CHAPTER 20: WHY, THEN, DO WOMEN NOT LEAD?

[1]Avivah Wittenberg-Cox, "Study: Female Executives Make Progress, but Mostly in Support Functions," *Harvard Business Review*, April 21, 2014, http://blogs.hbr.org/2014/04/study-female-executives-make-progress-but -mostly-in-support-functions.

[2]"A Quick Question: What Percentage of Pastors Are Female?," Hartford Institute for Religion Research, accessed September 18, 2014, http://hirr .hartsem.edu/research/quick_question3.html.

[3]A guide to some recent literature on these matters is provided by Jill Flynn, Kathryn Heath, and Mary Davis Holt, "Six Paradoxes Women Leaders Face in 2013," *Harvard Business Review*, January 3, 2013, http://blogs.hbr.org/2013 /01/six-paradoxes-women-leaders-fa.

[4]Jennifer L. Lawless and Richard L. Fox, "Why Are Women Still Not Running for Public Office?," *Governance Studies* 16 (May 2008).

[5]Jill Lapore, "The X Factor," *The New Yorker*, March 10, 2014, p. 22.

[6]It is intriguing in this regard to note the recent rise in "B corporations," "social entrepreneurship," and the like as more and more "workers—especially young ones—want to work for socially conscious companies, and will take less compensation in exchange for a greater sense of purpose." James Surowiecki, "Companies with Benefits," *The New Yorker*, August 4, 2014, p. 23.

[7]Lisa Belkin, "The Opt-Out Revolution," *The New York Times*, October 26, 2003, www.nytimes.com/2003/10/26/magazine/26WOMEN.html?page wanted=all.

[8]Linda Babcock and Sara Laschever, *Women Don't Ask: Negotiation and the Gender Divide* (Princeton, NJ: Princeton University Press, 2003).

[9]Virginia Valian, *Why So Slow? The Advancement of Women* (Boston: MIT Press, 1997).

[10]Katty Kay and Claire Shipman, "The Confidence Gap," *The Atlantic*, May 2014, p. 66; see also Katty Kay and Claire Shipman, *The Confidence Code: The Science and Art of Self-Assurance—What Women Should Know* (New York: HarperBusiness, 2014).

[11]Anna Fels, *Necessary Dreams: Ambition in Women's Changing Lives* (New York: Pantheon, 2004).

[12]Diane Swanbrow, "Exactly How Much Housework Does a Husband Create?," *University of Michigan News*, April 3, 2008, http://ns.umich.edu /new/releases/6452.

[13]Marianne Bertrand, Jessica Pan, and Emir Kamenica, "Gender Identity and Relative Income Within Households," National Bureau of Economic Research Working Paper No. 19023 (May 2013), http://nber.org/papers/w19023.

CHAPTER 21: HOW TO CHANGE A MIND

[1]In what follows, I borrow from my published testimony, "How to Produce an Egalitarian Man," in *How I Changed My Mind About Women in Leadership: Compelling Stories from Prominent Evangelicals*, ed. Alan F. Johnson (Grand Rapids: Zondervan, 2010), pp. 235-43.

[2]Virginia Valian, *Why So Slow? The Advancement of Women* (Boston: MIT Press, 1997).

[3]Thomas S. Kuhn, *The Structure of Scientific Revolutions*, 2nd ed. (Chicago: University of Chicago Press, 1970 [1962]).

Scripture Index

Finding the Textbook You Need

The IVP Academic Textbook Selector
is an online tool for instantly finding the IVP books
suitable for over 250 courses across 24 disciplines.

ivpacademic.com